'There are four reasons why you should read this boo
system is inevitably being transformed by technolog,
this book presents a coherent vision of a successor system that would be su-
perior to others currently on offer. Second, the system it describes is an answer to the perennial objection to eliminating nuclear weapons, which is that
there is no better way to prevent war: yes, there is, it says. Third, this book is
an encyclopaedic history of things you never knew before about world peace
through law and the 'practical men' like Teddy Roosevelt, who supported the
idea. And fourth, if you think ponderous prose goes with the territory on this
subject, think again: this book is engaging, lively, and fun.'

James Goodby, Chief U.S. Negotiator for the Safe and Secure
Dismantlement of Nuclear Weapons (1993)

'There is no problem more important than halting the illegal use of armed
force to settle international disputes. James Taylor Ranney's book offers the
readers a comprehensive historical analysis with possible solutions to contem-
poraneous conflicts. It is an invaluable goldmine for all students concerned
with current problems of world peace.'

Benjamin B. Ferencz,
Former Nuremberg War Crimes Prosecutor and Peace Advocate

'A powerful argument that the abolition of nuclear weapons requires a stronger
regime for the peaceful resolution of international disputes. Ranney marshals
compelling evidence that the world is moving in that direction in any case because of the need for peaceful solutions of the multiplying issues that are arising
in global markets and the global commons. The danger from nuclear weapons is
so acute, however, that this evolutionary process is insufficient. A more urgent,
focused effort is required.'

Frank N. von Hippel, Princeton University, USA

'Just when the vision of a world at peace seems to have faded into obscu-
rity, James Taylor Ranney comes along with an updated version of his classic
study 'Peace through Law'. It could also be titled 'Peace is Possible' and will
encourage visionaries and convert sceptics.'

Peter Weiss, President Emeritus,
International Association of Lawyers Against Nuclear Arms, USA

'This book is refreshing and a badly needed antidote at a time when hawks
with sinister faces tell us that peace and arms control can be threatened by
a convention that commits states to non-use and non-possession of nuclear
weapons. When the world is spending nearly two trillion dollars a year on
means and measures to blow us up, Professor Ranney has the temerity to argue for the ending of wars. He does not grope for a world federation or general
and complete disarmament, but rather for reliance on law and moderate and
time honoured means such as mediation, arbitration and UN forces.'

Hans Blix, Third Director-General Emeritus of the
International Atomic Energy Agency

'In this lively, creative challenge to war—and especially nuclear war—James
T. Ranney provides us with a path toward an international system governed
by law rather than by violence. Championing arms reductions and dispute

resolution, backed by effective enforcement, Ranney outlines a practical way to move toward a more peaceful world.'

Lawrence S. Wittner, author of Confronting the Bomb

'James Taylor Ranney's book straddles a number of subject areas in a creative and very readable fashion. It should be of interest to those interested in international relations, security studies, disarmament, peace studies, dispute resolution and, of course, international law and international organizations.'

Roger S. Clark, Rutgers University, USA

'On the basis of lifelong learning and deep ethical commitments, James Taylor Ranney has produced a comprehensive guide to how peace might be secured in our troubled times by a prudent reliance on the mechanisms, institutions, and values of law. Every engaged citizen has an obligation to read this book and ponder its central prescriptions for achieving a peaceful world.'

Richard Falk, Professor Emeritus, Princeton University, USA

'This new work merging history, political science, and jurisprudence is superbly clear, accessible and cogent not only for scholars and academics, but also for leaders and decision-makers in governmental and non-governmental organizations, and for all looking to become better informed on how to achieve and maintain peace through the global rule of law.'

Kevin Govern, Center for Ethics and the Rule of Law, USA

'In *World Peace Through Law* James Taylor Ranney thoughtfully proposes concrete measures that could lead countries to abolish nuclear weapons, establish compulsory international dispute settlement mechanisms, and create effective enforcement mechanisms, including an international police force. Carefully researched, the book analyzes the intellectual roots of the world peace through law concept and explores the efforts of activists and politicians – including many U.S. Presidents, both Democratic and Republican – to realize its core features. The world greatly needs Ranney's mix of idealism and pragmatism concerning how international law can further the essential goals of peace and security.'

John E. Noyes, Professor Emeritus, California Western School of Law, USA

'In this stimulating, thought-provoking, thoroughly researched, and historically grounded volume, James Taylor Ranney brings together his reflections on world peace through the rule of law carefully and systematically developed over the course of several decades. His argument and seriousness of purpose are enhanced throughout by his candid discussions of the counter- positions of those who disagree with him and his honest acknowledgment that there are 'many different paths to peace'. Ranney describes himself as a 'pragmatic idealist' who is realistic about the weaknesses of existing international law but at the same time optimistic about its future possibilities. Toward this end, he is owed a debt of gratitude for his vision of how the world might move toward future peace.'

Paul Gordon Lauren, University of Montana, USA

'James Taylor Ranney's book is an important contribution to raising awareness, deepening understanding, and inspiring a new generation of peace activists to campaign for lawful alternatives to organized armed violence around the globe.'

Mary Ellen O'Connell, University of Notre Dame, USA

World Peace Through Law

This book deals with the history and future of the concept of 'world peace through law' (WPTL), which advocates replacing the use of international force with the global rule of law.

WPTL calls for replacing war with the global rule of law by arms reductions, including the abolition of nuclear weapons, global alternative dispute resolution mechanisms, and various enforcement mechanisms. This book sets forth a three-part proposal: (1) arms reductions—primarily the abolition of nuclear weapons, with necessarily concomitant reductions in conventional forces; (2) a four-stage system of global alternative dispute resolution (ADR), utilizing both law and equity; (3) adequate enforcement mechanisms, including a UN Peace Force. The core of this proposal is alternative dispute resolution mechanisms—international ADR. International ADR would consist of a four-stage process of compulsory negotiation, compulsory mediation, compulsory arbitration, and compulsory adjudication by the World Court. The fundamental proposition of this book is that the use of alternatives to war, global ADR, is the ultimate solution to the problem of peace. The full implementation of WPTL will entail a vast array of progressive initiatives on many fronts, including the abolition of nuclear weapons, with the global rule of law being the capstone to all of these developments.

This book will be of great interest to students of peace studies, arms control, international law, and world politics.

James Taylor Ranney is a retired Adjunct Professor, Widener Law School, USA. He was a co-founder of the Jeannette Rankin Peace Center, a Legal Consultant to the United Nations International Criminal Tribunal for the Former Yugoslavia, Chair of the Philadelphia Chapter of Citizens for Global Solutions, and is currently a Board Member of the Project for Nuclear Awareness.

World Peace Through Law

Replacing War with the Global
Rule of Law

James Taylor Ranney

Routledge
Taylor & Francis Group

LONDON AND NEW YORK

First published 2018 by Routledge

2 Park Square, Milton Park, Abingdon, Oxfordshire OX14 4RN

52 Vanderbilt Avenue, New York, NY 10017

Routledge is an imprint of the Taylor & Francis Group, an informa business

First issued in paperback 2019

British Library Cataloguing-in-Publication Data
A catalogue record for this book is available from the British Library

Library of Congress Cataloging-in-Publication Data
Names: Ranney, James T., author.
Title: World peace through law: replacing war with the global rule of law / James Taylor Ranney.
Description: Abingdon, Oxon; New York, NY: Routledge, 2018. | Includes bibliographical references and index.
Identifiers: LCCN 2017032216 | ISBN 9781138563643 (hardback) | ISBN 9781315121864 (ebook)
Subjects: LCSH: Pacific settlement of international disputes. | Rule of law. | Arbitration (International law) | Pacific settlement of international disputes—History—20th century.
Classification: LCC KZ6010 .R366 2018 | DDC 341.5/22—dc23
LC record available at https://lccn.loc.gov/2017032216

ISBN: 978-1-138-56364-3 (hbk)
ISBN: 978-0-367-23299-3 (pbk)

Typeset in Times New Roman
by codeMantra

This book is dedicated to my wife, Harriett Elaine Frazey Ranney, without whose steadfast support I could not have written this book, and to my grandchildren, August Kao Ranney and Amara Kao Ranney.

Contents

x   *Contents*

Acknowledgments

I would like to single out a few of the many persons whose work on the peace issue have been particularly helpful: Professor Paul Gordon Lauren, Mansfield Professor of Ethics and Public Policy at the University of Montana, who guided my early reading on the peace issue back in 1983; Professor Burns Weston, University of Iowa Law School, whose 1990 collection of essays *Alternative Security: Living Without Nuclear Deterrence* was used in my Contemporary Legal Problems Seminar "Law and World Peace" in 1986 and 1987; Benjamin Ferencz, who gave me a free copy of his book *Common Sense and World Peace*; Admiral Gene LaRocque, then president of the Center for Defense Information, who gave me a line-by-line critique of my 1983 "Many Paths to Peace" slideshow transcript; Patricia Mische (met at 1984 conference), whose book *Toward a Human World Order* has been a classic to many of us; Roger Molander, who also graciously critiqued my slideshow transcript and whose wonderful little 1982 paper-book *Nuclear War: What's In It For You?* I used to sell at cost; Robert Muller, whose books have been an inspiration to thousands of us (had the great pleasure of meeting him up at the UN in April 2005); Randall Forsberg (met at 2005 MIT conference), who was perhaps the best strategic thinker on the peace issue in America; Jonathan Schell, whose book *The Fate of the Earth* was for many of us the beginning of our quests for world peace; Professor Louis Sohn, whose many writings have obviously informed my work; Jonathan Granoff, my friend and colleague team-teaching International Law and an Advanced International Law Seminar; and finally, the late Vince Della Penna, whom I used to consult daily on this issue.

Preface

The proposal for lasting peace set forth in the following pages is simple—world peace through law—replacing the international use of force (war) with the global rule of law. The basic concept is neither new nor radical. It is merely an updated version of "world peace through law" (WPTL) proposals that have been made or endorsed over the years by five American presidents—Ulysses S. Grant, Teddy Roosevelt, William Howard Taft, Dwight D. Eisenhower, and John F. Kennedy. The basic components of our updated version of WPTL are: (1) arms reductions (including abolition of nuclear weapons), not general and complete disarmament; (2) global alternative dispute resolution systems, not world government or world federalism; and (3) viable enforcement mechanisms (including an international police force), not pacifism. In short, it is a very moderate proposal. Indeed, the core idea—the global rule of law—is merely an extension of the basic American idea. That is why it is surprising that it has been almost completely neglected over the past half century.[1]

The current neglect of the WPTL concept has been accompanied by similar neglect of the nuclear war and peace issue in recent years. As stated by Jonathan Schell:

> [A] new post-Cold War generation, largely innocent of nuclear knowledge, was growing up. Its elders, having dropped the nuclear issue themselves, also forgot to impart even the most basic information regarding nuclear matters to their children. The press neglected the issue, as did schools at every level. And so to elderly amnesia was added an ocean of fresh, young, pure ignorance.[2]

The reasons for this neglect are manifold:

> When the Cold War abruptly ended with the dissolution of the Soviet Union, anti-nuclear activists and ordinary people everywhere

collectively breathed a huge sigh of relief, hoping and believing that they had walked away from a nuclear holocaust and putting nuclear weapons out of their minds ... Meanwhile, deeply imbedded in the US military-industrial-academic complex, the nuclear juggernaut rolled on, as militarists in the Pentagon and scientists at the nuclear weapons labs conjured up new justifications to project the nuclear weapons enterprise into the future ... During the 1990's, nuclear weapons—especially US nuclear weapons—disappeared from the public's radar screen. Questions of nuclear arms control, non-proliferation, and disarmament became increasingly isolated from issues of concern to most ordinary people—including issues of war and peace—and increasingly relegated to elite policy circles inside the Washington, DC beltway.[3]

Part of the reason for this dearth of academic course offerings and public discussion is the difficulty of finding a faculty or others who combine the requisite areas of expertise. As stated by James Doyle, a former researcher at a nuclear lab:

The need for understanding of today's evolving nuclear threats is critical to informing policy decisions and diplomacy that can move the world toward greater nuclear security. The scientific underpinnings for such an understanding are remarkably broad, ranging from nuclear physics and engineering to chemistry, metallurgy and materials science, risk assessment, large-scale computational techniques, modeling and simulation, and detector development, among others. These physical science disciplines must be combined with social science fields such as public policy, political science, international relations, international law, energy policies, economics, history, and regional studies in order to yield a deep understanding of today's nuclear security challenges.[4]

I believe that I have accumulated a unique combination of knowledge and expertise relevant to the peace issue and that this book contributes to an understanding of this important problem. Nevertheless, no specialized knowledge or training is necessary to fully understand this book.

Notes

1 See John E. Noyes, "William Howard Taft and the Taft Arbitration Treaties," 56 *Vill. L. Rev.* 535, 552 (2011)("the view that international arbitration or an international court can assure the peaceful settlement of disputes between rival states has largely disappeared.") and Mark Mazower, Governing the World: The History of an Idea, at 86 (2012)

(international arbitration idea "has remained in the shadows" after a flurry of activity in late 19th and early 20th centuries). Of the dozens of syllabi for college courses in conflict resolution I have seen, none deal with WPTL.

2 Jonathan Schell, The Seventh Decade: The New Shape of Nuclear Danger, at 11 (2007).

3 Ray Acheson, ed., Beyond Arms Control: Challenges and Choices for Nuclear Disarmament, at 127–128 (2010). See also Douglas Roche, How We Stopped Loving the Bomb: An Insider's Account of the World on the Brink of Banning Nuclear Arms, at 161 (2011)("Generally, throughout high school and even in colleges and universities, academic curricula barely touch nuclear disarmament, school boards and administrators considering the subject too 'political' for the classroom. The result of this starvation diet is a woefully uninformed public, which, of course, seldom raises the nuclear issues with politicians.") and Tanya Ogilvie-White and David Santoro, Slaying the Nuclear Dragon: Disarmament Dynamics in the Twenty-First Century, at 8 (2012)(nuclear education programs no longer "fashionable").

4 James E. Doyle, "National Security as a Multidisciplinary Field of Study, at 1–2 (2008). See also Katie Bacon, "Double Strength: A New Collaboration between HLS and Brookings Takes on Security Issues," *Harvard Law Bulletin* (Wtr, 2012), at 24 (in order to properly address these issues "you need expertise in constitutional law, in foreign relations, in criminal law, in human rights, in religion and in technology"). Additionally, it would be helpful to have expertise in alternative dispute resolution (including arbitration and mediation), archeology and anthropology, environmental studies, diplomatic and evolutionary and legal and military history, peace studies, political psychology, security studies, and social change theory.

1 The problem

It is not enough that their elders promise 'Peace in our time'; it must be peace in their time too, and in their children's time; indeed, my friends, there is only one real peace now, and that is **peace for all time**.
—Dwight David Eisenhower

Whether we realize it or not, the most important issue facing humanity—more important than the dangers of terrorism and nuclear proliferation—is how to avoid a nuclear war between the superpowers, a war with "the potential to destroy all civilisation and the entire eco-system of the planet" in a single day.[1]

It will be immediately objected that such an untoward possibility is simply unthinkable, that nobody would be stupid enough to start WWIII, so why worry about it. One problem with this objection is that it neglects our historical experience in regard to starting world wars, specifically WWI. Prior to WWI, there were several statements by the leading experts of the time that "no nation would be so foolish as to start [a war]," that "new economic factors clearly prove the inanity of aggressive wars," and that given the awesome armaments in existence even then war was altogether quite "unthinkable."[2] Of course, despite these authoritative pronouncements, we know what happened.[3]

What could possibly go wrong?

Moreover, consider the following:

1   On the evening of October 25, 1962, at the height of the Cuban Missile Crisis, an air force sentry at a military base near Duluth, Minnesota "spotted someone climbing the base fence, shot at the

figure, and sounded the sabotage alarm." As alarms at airfields all over the region were sounded, at Volk Field, Wisconsin, the wrong alarm, the one signaling nuclear war (the "P.S., we mean it, this is not a drill" alarm) went off, and pilots scrambled and headed down the runway, being stopped only at the last second by the post commander. The "intruder" was a bear.[4]

2   Also in the midst of the Cuban Missile Crisis, only two days later, October 27, 1962, on the same day that an American U-2 spy plane was shot down over Cuba: At this point, Soviet submarines were being subjected to depth charges to make them rise to the surface (we were unaware they had nuclear weapons aboard). Despite strict orders not to use their nuclear torpedoes absent authorization from Moscow, the three Soviet officers aboard Foxtrot submarine B-59 had decided to use theirs if under attack and unable to reach Moscow but only if all three officers agreed. They were, in fact, unable to reach Moscow, and in the end, one officer, *Vasili Alexandrovich Arkipov*, finally made the fateful decision not to start WWIII.[5]

3   In 1983, U.S.-NATO military maneuvers in Europe, called "Able Archer 83," were interpreted for a time by the Soviets as the prelude to a—not so good—full-scale nuclear attack.[6]

4   On January 25, 1995, technicians at the Olengrosk early warning radar facility detected an unidentified ballistic missile over Norway which appeared to be heading for Russia. Because the missile was manufactured in the United States, its "signature trail" was therefore identified by Russian computers as hostile and apparently fired from a U.S. submarine in the Arctic Sea, even though it was actually only a *Norwegian research rocket researching the Northern Lights*. President Yeltsen's "nuclear briefcase" was activated and Russian missile submarines ordered to battle stations. Finally, with three minutes to spare, the missile was correctly identified.[7] Happily, for the human race, this incident took place at a time when Yeltsin was President and not earlier (or subsequent) presidents.

But this is the mere tip of the iceberg of close calls known to experts. There have been literally hundreds of false alerts of a nuclear attack in this country alone, triggered by such things as a flock of geese, the rising of the moon, the sun's reflection on a cloud, a strong solar storm, and space debris re-entering the atmosphere.[8] And of course, there have been who knows how many similar or worse incidents in other countries, with their less than adequate detection and warning devices.[9] In short, it is only because we have been incredibly lucky that we have not already had an accidental nuclear war thus far.[10] Anytime you can come as close to WWIII as we have come on more than one occasion, it is only a matter of time before nuclear weapons will be used—either by accident or miscalculation or in what might be called a "pre-preemptive preventive strike." Famed Cold War warrior Paul Nitze explains the danger of such a strike, where one country is anticipating a pre-emptive first strike by another,

> might well feel it should strike even sooner than planned to head off [the other country's] preemptive blow. I could foresee the possibility of a situation arising in which there would be such an interaction of fear that it would be almost impossible to conceive how statesmen could prevent the situation from deteriorating into war.[11]

For those who think that all these concerns are now quite dated after the alleged end of the Cold War, consider this recent news item:

> MOSCOW—A senior Russian general [Nikolai Makarov] on Wednesday threatened preemptive attacks on missile-defense sites in Poland and elsewhere in Eastern Europe in the event of a crisis, underscoring the Kremlin's opposition to the Obama administration's plans [for missile defense] and further undermining relations between the countries.[12]

Even though this statement is most likely only a bluff, it nevertheless points out the kinds of dangers that could easily lead to an all-consuming humanity-annihilating world war.[13] These are some of the reasons that people like former Secretary of Defense William J. Perry said that "[t]he danger of a nuclear catastrophe today… is greater than it was during the Cold War."[14]

In sum, if one looks objectively at (a) the things we have done incompetently over the years (e.g., WWI, Three Mile Island, Chernobyl, Fukushima Daiichi, Gulf Oil Spill, Katrina, Challenger, etc.)[15] and (b) the things we have done deliberately (e.g., just in the years surrounding WWII: Guernica, the Rape of Nanking, Katyn Forest, Einsatzgruppen, Majdanek, Auschwitz, Buchenwald, Dachau, Belsen, Dresden, Tokyo, Hiroshima, Nagasaki, etc.[16]), it leaves one with little confidence in our ability to avoid what would be the ultimate disaster: a pointless Clausewitzian *Vernichtungsschlacht* ("battle of [mutual] annihilation").

Perhaps this paints too stark a picture of our prospects. Indeed, we will argue in a future chapter that there are many positive trends which counterbalance the above facts from our recent past. In any event, it strikes many of the most thoughtful and perceptive thinkers of the Nuclear Age that our current posture of "mutual assured destruction" is simply "too frightful and dangerous a way to live indefinitely."[17] For just as "ordinary deterrence" fails on a regular basis, so too nuclear deterrence is likely to someday fail.[18]

A little perspective

We need to be clear about what is at stake: all human life. Humanity is the culmination of an awesome evolutionary process that makes us kin not only to all other humans but also to the rocks and trees. We are told that the so-called Big Bang took place 13.8-billion years ago. Our Earth coalesced into existence about 4.58-billion years ago. The first life on earth—possibly, scientists now think, inside of the micro-porous membranes of alkaline hydrothermal vents—appears about 3.5-billion years ago.[19] The wildly diverse life forms of the Burgess Shale (in Canada, and now similar finds in Africa and China) are dated to around 560-million years ago. The first amphibians climbed onto dry land 365-million years ago; the first "true mammals" appeared about 200-million years ago; the earliest hominid: 4.5-million years ago. A new find, Australopithecus Sediba, believed to be an early ancestor of humans, with ape-like arms, but human teeth and legs, were dated 2-million years ago. Homo Sapiens: 300,000 years ago. The first human settlements and agriculture: 10,000 years ago. The first use of writing: 5,000 years ago.[20] And only in the last few hundred years: all the products of the great scientific and enlightenment revolutions (and the follow-on industrial and nuclear revolutions).[21] It appears that a succession of miracles were necessary for us to get where we are today, e.g.: the recently-discovered "Theia Collision Event," occurring during what scientists call the 30-million-year Titanomachean ("war of the planets") Period. During this period the Mars-sized planet Theia collided with the early Earth, eliminating Theia and almost destroying Earth while ejecting what became the moon, thereby adding just enough iron to the Earth's core to create the magnetic fields which prevent the solar winds from wiping out Earth's atmosphere and water. The moon itself, which stabilized Earth's axial tilt, thereby allowing a moderate climate to develop. Next came the "Water from Outer Space Era," starting several billion years ago, when water and ice-laden comets and meteorites jarred loose from their orbits by destabilization of the outer planets were caught by Earth's gravity and inundated the planet with just enough water to sustain life but not so much as to create a Water World that would have precluded a technological civilization. The Great Oxidation Event, was next, starting 2.4 billion years ago, when, for whatever reason or reasons, oxygen levels gradually increased from almost nothing to where it now constitutes 21% of our atmosphere, allowing complex life forms to exist. The Ozone Layer Creation Era, came about 600 million years ago, when oxygen high up in the atmosphere absorbed energy and split into single oxygen atoms, which then combined with regular oxygen to form ozone, which has the happy characteristic of blocking 98% of ultraviolet radiation, thereby allowing plants and animals to survive. Next was the "Mexican Meteorite" event, 66 million years ago, causing the extinction of the dinosaurs and allowing mammals to flourish. Finally, the Domestication of the Fire Revolution; cooking causing bigger brains, increased male-female bonding, and sociality.[22] In short, for all our faults, we are nothing short of a miracle of evolution, standing at the edge of history, a history which should be allowed to continue.[23]

Notes

1 *Legality of the Threat or Use of Nuclear Weapons*, ICJ Advisory Opinion, para. 36, UN Document A/51/218 (July 8, 1996). While politicians spend most of their time talking about the threats of terrorism and nuclear proliferation, consider the relative threats from these dangers vis a vis a human-life-terminating WWIII. While the former threats realistically threaten at most hundreds of thousands of lives, the latter existential threat threatens not only the billions of existing lives but all the literally trillions upon trillions of future lives which would be occasioned by human extinction. It's true that one needs to factor in the likelihood of such an event occurring. But let's do that. If the odds of the former kind of attacks (terrorists and proliferators) are even as high as 100% over the next decade, when you multiply the projected deaths (rounding upward to an even million) times the odds, you get an overall product of 1,000,000. Since the risk of nuclear Armageddon cannot be less than one in a thousand over that same time period, cf. Martin E. Hellman, "How risky is nuclear optimism?," 67 *Bulletin of the Atomic Scientists* 47 (2011), multiplying projected deaths (rounding down to a mere one trillion) times the odds (.001) yields a product of 1,000,000,000, which happens to be precisely one thousand times as great as the former product. But which topic is more often discussed by public officials? The former. In sum, the existential threat is a very serious one that needs to be seriously addressed.

2 Barbara W. Tuchman, The Guns of August, at 10 (1962). Cf. also "The world in 1913: The year before the sky fell in," *Economist*, June 8, 2013, at 85 (The *Economist* in June of 1913 found world trends "slowly but surely making war between the civilized communities of the world an

impossibility"). Some political science/international relations scholars argue once again that major war is now obsolete. See, e.g., John Mueller, Retreat from Doomsday: The Obsolescence of Major War (1989). For the reasons which follow in the text, this thesis is every bit as wrong as the pre-WWI predictions.

3 See G.J. Meyer, A World Undone: The Story of the Great War 1914 to 1918, Chapters 3–6 (2006) (an astonishing tale of miscues, miscommunications, misunderstandings, and blunders lead to war) and Margaret MacMillan, The War That Ended Peace: The Road to 1914 (2013) (definitive work). Cf. Margaret MacMillan, "The Rhyme of History: Lessons of the Great War," *Brookings Brief* (December 14, 2013) (uncanny parallels between 1914 and now). Cf. also Michael Howard, The Franco-Prussian War, at 57 (1961) ("Thus, by a tragic combination of ill luck, stupidity, and ignorance, France blundered into war....").

4 Michael O'Hanlon, A Skeptic's Case for Nuclear Disarmament, at 36–37 (2010). The author, born and raised in Wisconsin, did not learn of this incident until 2012.

5 Michael Krepon, Better Safe Than Sorry: The Ironies of Living with the Bomb, at 36 (2009). See Niall Ferguson, The War of the World: Twentieth-Century Conflict and the Descent of the West, at 600–604 (2006) (other amazing details, inter alia: key military officials and McNamara had urged invasion, not knowing that 80 nuclear-armed missiles were ready to fire); Winslow Myers, Living Beyond War: A Citizen's Guide, at 40–41 (2009) (McNamara: "The actions of all three parties were shaped by misjudgments, miscalculations, and misinformation. In a nuclear age, such mistakes could be disastrous ... Therefore, we must achieve crisis avoidance") (emphasis added); Jo Fidgen, "Cuban missile crisis: When nuclear war seemed inevitable," *BBC* (October 24, 2012), www.bbc.co.uk/news/magazine-20068265 (very evocative insider stories); and Martin Hellman, "Fifty Years after the Cuban Missile Crisis: Time to Stop Bluffing at Nuclear Poker" (Briefing Paper, Federation of American Scientists, October, 2012(other astonishing risks of crisis).

6 Tad Daley, Apocalypse Never: Forging the Path to a Nuclear Weapons-Free World, at 90 (2010) and Henry Chancellor, Dir., "Soviet War Scare 1983" documentary (2007) (horrifying details).

7 Commander Robert Green, Security without Nuclear Deterrence, at 120–121 (2010).

8 See, e.g., Daley, supra, at 69 ("One Defense Department count listed 563 incidents of nuclear mistakes, malfunctions, and false alarms"). See id. at 68 (on September 26, 1983, Soviet Lieutenant Colonel Stanislav Petrov saw what appeared on his computer screen to be a full-scale nuclear attack and only because he violated his instructions to alert higher authorities to initiate launch-on-warning procedures was WWIII narrowly avoided); Jonathan Granoff, "The Process of Zero," *World Policy Journal*, 85, 86–87 (Wtr 2009/2010) (at 3 a.m., November 9, 1979, computers at three U.S. military command centers all showed 2200 incoming missiles; with a "few minutes" to spare, error was discovered to be a "training tape" mistakenly inserted into a computer); and Paul Bracken, The Second Nuclear Age: Strategy, Danger, and the New Power Politics, at 88 (2012) (the author helped prepare nuclear war games during Reagan administration, and learned that several

games "went nuclear" not because anybody went crazy, "but because they faithfully implemented the prevailing U.S. strategy" in the face of a crisis not foreseen).

9 See James E. Cartwright & Vladimir Dvorkin, "How to Avert a Nuclear War," *New York Times*, Op-Ed, April 19, 2015 (Russia's early warning satellites "stopped functioning last fall"; early warning systems of both sides depend upon computers, in an era of increasing cyberwarfare) and Theodore Postol, "There are higher chances of accidental nuclear war now than during the Cold War," www.youtube.com/watch?v:GbrfR2yrsEE#t=151 (April 20, 2015) (fact that Russia now has to rely upon line-of-sight radars makes for dangerous situation where Russian leaders may have to assume the worst based on limited information; new fuses on Trident missiles makes them twice as destructive, thereby increasing Russian hair-trigger tendency).

10 See William J. Perry, My Journey at the Nuclear Brink, at 3 (2015) ("Although the Cuban Missile Crisis ended without war, I believed then, and still believe, that the world avoided a nuclear holocaust as much by good luck as by good management") and Gregg Herken, Counsels of War, at 165 (1985) (JFK estimated odds of nuclear war during 13-day crisis at 50% [this was prior to revelations showing danger was much greater than realized at the time]).

11 Mike Moore, Twilight War: The Folly of U.S. Space Dominance, at 336 n. 27 (2008) (emphasis added). See also Robert E. Berls, Jr. & Leon Ratz, Rising Nuclear Dangers: Assessing the Risk of Nuclear Use in the Euro-Atlantic Region (Nuclear Threat Initiative, October 2015) (10 factors analyzed: competing irreconcilable narratives that heightened threat perceptions; deficit of trust; domestic political imperatives; alliance politics; close military encounters; broken channels of communication; failing safeguards to prevent nuclear use; conventional force disparity; reckless nuclear saber rattling; and lack of nuclear experience).

12 *Philadelphia Inquirer*, May 4, 2012, p. A6: "Russian general threatens NATO missile shield." See also Stephen F. Cohen, Soviet Fates and Lost Alternatives: From Stalinism to the New Cold War, at 168–181 (2010) (due to "triumphalist" policies, such as NATO expansion, withdrawal from ABM Treaty, and urging regime change, risks of military conflict greater than ever).

13 Cf. also *Philadelphia Inquirer*, August 6, 2009, p. A3: "Russian official: Sub patrols off U.S. are routine" (re-establishing sub and bomber patrols, which had been terminated for over a decade). Plus, this does not count the nuclear submarines of China and potentially (absent abolition) other countries, which can be stationed minutes off our shores. See, e.g., Anthony Capaccio & David Tweed, "U.S. Says Chinese Sub That Can Hit U.S. on Patrol Soon," *Bloomberg News* September 24, 2015 (new sub, joining four others, has range of 4600 miles and can hit all 50 states from east of Hawaii) and Joseph S. Bermudez, Jr., "North Korea's SINPO-class Sub: New Evidence of Possible Vertical Missile Launch Tubes; Sinpo Shipyard Prepares for Significant Naval Construction Program," *38 North* January 14, 2015.

14 Ira Helfand, Andy Haines, Tilman Ruff, Hans Kristensen, Patricia Lewis, & Zia Mian, "The Growing Threat of Nuclear War and the Role of the Health Community," 2 *World Medical Journal* 86 (2016).

15 Not to mention the many incidents specifically involving nuclear weapons. See Eric Schlosser, Command and Control (2013) (detailing hundreds of appalling mistakes and accidents, often hidden from the public and even other government officials). Also, cf. Mark A. Stokes, "Securing Nuclear Arsenals: A Chinese Case Study," Chapter 3 in Henry D. Sokolski & Bruno Tertrais, eds., Nuclear Weapons Security Crises: What Does History Teach? (2013) (China's near loss of control of nuclear arsenal during Cultural Revolution).
16 See Andrew Roberts, The Storm of War: A New History of the Second World War (2011) (numerous other atrocities, e.g., Bydgoszcz, Piotrkow, Wormhout, Lidice, Oradour-sur-Glane and Theresianstadt); Michael Burleigh, Moral Combat: Good and Evil in World War II, at xvi–xvii, 397–403 (2011) (Chelmno, Maly Trostenets, Sajmiste, Telechany, Hancewicze, Janow, Borodice, Lohiszyn, Pinsk, Dawidgorodek, Kamenetz-Podolsk); Nicholas Stargardt, The German War: A Nation under Arms: Citizens and Soldiers, 1939–1945, at 41–45, 163, 172–174, 234, 244, 516 (2015) (Piasnica/Neustadt, Szpedawsk, Koeborowoi, Gruppa, Lszkowko, Mniszek, Miedzyn, Rusinowo, Karlhof, Bromberg/Bydgoszcz, Lvov, Riga, Kaunas, Belaia Tserkov, Stanislau, Mittelban-Dora, and Neuengamme); Timothy Snyder, Black Earth: The Holocaust as History and Warning (2015) (hundreds of other death sites).
17 Herbert York, "Reducing the Overkill," 16 *Survival* 2 (March/April 1974) (York was a Manhattan Project physicist who was director of defense research under President Eisenhower and the first director of Lawrence Livermore National Laboratory).
18 See Ward Wilson, "Myth, Hiroshima and Fear: How We Overestimated the Usefulness of the Bomb," 1 *CADMUS Journal* 145, 148 (2012).
19 Nick Lane, The Vital Question: Why is Life the Way It Is? (2015) (life made from three simple ingredients—rocks [olivine, containing ferrous sulfide needed in ion exchange], water, and carbon dioxide—via electrochemical reactions across the membranes).
20 See Stanislaus Dehaene, Reading in the Brain: The Science and Evolution of a Human Invention (2009). Also cf. Philip Lieberman, The Unpredictable Species: What Makes Humans Unique (2013) (astonishing evolutionary neurobiological history of human development of capacity for speech ca. 200,000 years ago).
21 Cf. Jay Minik, The Great Upheaval: America and the Birth of the Modern World, 1788–1800 (2007) (arguing that the 1790s was "the decade that made the modern world," building upon the works of Hobbes, Locke, Rousseau, Milton, Newton, Vivaldi and Bach) and James T. Ranney, "Heritage of Our Freedoms" Slideshow Transcript, at 36–43 (1987) (also referring to Mozart, Beethoven, Haydn, Goethe, Kant, Lavoisie, and the men behind the U.S. Constitution [1787], with its core values of democracy, equality, freedom, and the rule of law).
22 See Richard Wrangham, Catching Fire: How Cooking Made Us Human (2009) (campfires found as old as 790,000 years ago).
23 Significantly, cultural evolution takes place much faster than biological evolution. See Matt Ridley, The Evolution of Everything: How Ideas Emerge, at 28–33 (2015) (proof that morality evolves). Also, cf. Carter Phipps, Evolutionaries: Unlocking the Spiritual and Cultural Potential of Science's Greatest Idea (2012) (the belief that there is a "moral purpose" to the Universe, working itself out by a process of cosmic evolution).

2   The answer

The crux of the "world peace through law" idea can be stated simply: some comprehensive and effective dispute-settlement machinery to resolve all forms of international conflict, backed up with effective enforcement mechanisms.

The basic logic behind WPTL consists of this syllogistic argument: there are only two ways to resolve conflict at the international level: (1) by war, and (2) by law. Therefore, choose the law, the only question becoming precisely what do we mean by "law," i.e., what kind of "law" will it take in order to replace the use of force with the rule of law at the international level?

World federalists argue that only "world law" will suffice, defined as law generated by a global parliament and enforced by a global judiciary and executive.[1] World federalists argue that existing "international law" and international legal institutions are weak and inadequate. They (and their polar opposites, the neo-conservatives) are right about that. Existing international law[2] does tend to be too vague, fragmentary, and lacking in adequate enforcement mechanisms.[3] As stated by Professor Eric Posner:

> Thus, international legal institutions seem to be exceptionally thin and unbalanced—as though, to use a domestic analogy, the U.S. Congress made laws only by unanimous rule, U.S. courts could hear cases but not enforce their judgments or even compel litigants to appear before them, and no executive existed and instead people relied on self-help to enforce their rights. Such a system would seem to be a recipe for anarchy[4]

And while many international legal scholars have done a fine job of defending international law from some of the more intemperate attacks of today's neo-conservatives,[5] they often slide over the uncomfortable fact that the ultimate "sanctions" of current international law (aside from international opinion) are reprisals and war.[6] Furthermore, even if it is true, as famously stated by Louis Henkin, that "[a]lmost all nations observe almost all principles of international law and almost all of their obligations almost all of the time,"[7] almost all of the time is obviously inadequate in the age of nuclear weapons. We must do better than existing international law.

What is the answer? Must we await the millennial moment when world federalism supposedly finally arrives? Is the status quo satisfactory, with its UN-based system of "collective insecurity," buttressed by the United States bleeding itself white to play World Cop? Is it true that "[our] current institutions do not work, and no practicable alternative can likely work"[8]? Can our Best and Brightest of the usual academic and other establishment elites do no better, after a three-year Princeton-sponsored series of conferences, than the idea for a so-called "Concert of Democracies"?[9] Is there anything to overcome the sense of "malaise" now felt by most reform-minded internationalists?[10] Is there an answer to Harvard Law Professor David Kennedy's excellent question: "Our common project is governance: how can sovereign states be governed so that war may be avoided?"[11] I submit that there is an answer: it is the old and long-forgotten idea called "world peace through law," updated to take cognizance of the world in which we now live and the world we are about to enter.

The twenty-first-century version of WPTL proposed is a collection of several key concepts, none of them original, but collectively perhaps a new idea: (1) certain specified arms reductions (primarily abolition of nuclear weapons, with concomitant reductions in conventional forces that would necessarily accompany an abolition convention); (2) a four-stage system of global alternative dispute resolution; and (3) various enforcement mechanisms, including an international peace force. Although we will retain the classic terminology of "world peace through law," we will not be using the traditional definition of "law," which would limit it to existing international law. Rather, our more comprehensive view of law will differ in two major respects: (1) we will include within our definition of law all the alternative dispute resolution mechanisms, such as mediation and arbitration, which until recently were not recognized as being part of law at all; and (2) we will permit even the adjudicative stage of our international dispute resolution system to make full use of equity.

Our updated version of WPTL will steer a path in-between the world federalists and the "global legalists," a path in-between alternatives that are either way too much or way too little. Our proposal is a practical non-utopian idea that can be accomplished in the relative near term and, contrary to the assumptions of many, all without creating a global legislature, or adopting general and complete disarmament.

Notes

1 The world federalists were very popular in the 1940s, with prominent members such as Albert Einstein and Bertrand Russell, but with the McCarthy Era their numbers dropped precipitately and have remained rather low ever since. See generally Joseph Preston Baratta, The Politics of World Federation (2004) (tracing the history of world federalism back to ancient times); Lawrence S. Wittner, One World or None: A History of the World Nuclear Disarmament Movement through 1953 (1993); Christopher Hamer, A Global Parliament: Principles of World Federalism (1998) (excellent exposition of principles); and Grenville Clark and Louis Sohn, World Peace Through World Law (3rd ed. 1966) (the classic work, with a detailed proposal). Cf. also Inis Claude, Swords into Plowshares: The Problems and Progress of International Organization, Chapters 18 & 19 (4th ed. 1971) (brilliant critique of world federalism).

2 Do not look for a definition of this term; it is not a treatise on international law. But cf. Mark W. Janis, America and the Law of Nations 1776–1939, at 20–21 (2010) (offering up various definitions). Similarly, do not look for my views to fall into any particular academic school of thought regarding international law. They do not. I am simply a pragmatic idealist—realistic about the weaknesses of existing international law, but optimistic about its future possibilities.

3 See, e.g., Benjamin B. Ferencz, "A World of Peace under the Rule of Law: The View from America," 6 *Wash. U. Global Studies L. Rev.* 664, 664 (2007) ("And in the international arena, all of these components [law, courts, and enforcement] are very weak. The laws are uncertain and ambiguous. International courts such as the International Court of Justice, have no independent enforcement powers").

4 Eric A. Posner, "International Law: A Welfarist Approach," 73 *U. Chi. L. Rev.* 487, 540 (2006).

5 See, e.g., Mary Ellen O'Connell, The Power and Purpose of International Law: Insights from the Theory and Practice of Enforcement (2008); Jens David Ohlin, The Assault on International Law (2015); and Paul Schiff Berman, "Seeing Beyond the Limits of International Law," 84 *Tex. L. Rev.* 1265 (2006). See also Antonio Augusto Cancado Trindade, International Law for Humankind: Towards a New *Jus Gentium* (2010) (more human-centered as opposed to state-centric perspective on international law).

6 Cf., e.g., O'Connell, supra, at 4–8. But cf. Ohlin, at 162 (modern uncertainty re law of reprisals).

7 Louis Henkin, How Nations Behave, at 47 (1979).

8 Michael J. Glennon, "Platonism, Adaptivism, and Illusion in UN Reform," 6 *Chi. J. Int'l Law* 613, 638 (2006) (cf. id. at 639: "The Security Council cannot prevent unwanted uses of force, and nothing useful can be put in its place").

9 Widely panned by virtually everyone once it saw the light of day. See, e.g., Thomas Carothers, "A League of Their Own," Foreign Policy (July/August 2008), at 44. See also Foreign Policy, Letters, at 9–10 (August/September 2008) (remarkably weak replies to attacks by Carothers). Cf. also "Concert of Democracies: A Seductive Sound," *Economist*, June 9, 2007, at 68–69 (Russian editor views proposal, not surprisingly, as creating a world "doomed to war").

10 Cf. David W. Kennedy, "A New World Order: Yesterday, Today, and Tomorrow," 4 *Transnat. L. & Contemp. Probs.* 329, 331 (1994). Cf. id. at 342 (current reform ideas "rarely specify a coherent overall blueprint for world peace").

11 David Kennedy, "One, Two, Three, Many Legal Orders: Legal Pluralism and the Cosmopolitan Dream," 31 *NYU Rev. L. & Soc. Change* 640, 650 (2007).

3   Bentham (1789)

Jeremy Bentham (1728–1832) is a famous British legal philosopher and social reformer perhaps best known as a proponent of the utilitarian doctrine of "the greatest good for the greatest number."[1] His work on the peace issue, however, is little known, at least in the United States.

When he set out to write *Plan for an Universal and Perpetual Peace*, Bentham could easily have simply chosen to adopt one of the models of world federalism that had been proposed in the late seventeenth century. Instead, he came up with a new idea. Finished in 1789, the year George Washington was sworn in as president of the United States, Bentham's Plan begins on a characteristic Jeremy Bentham self-assured note: "A proposal of this sort is one of those things that can never come too early nor too late."[2] After some entertaining discussion of "the madness" and "extreme folly" of war,[3] the crux of Bentham's proposal for a "general and complete pacification of all Europe" is a tripartite scheme: (1) troop reductions, especially in naval forces;[4] (2) "establishment of a Common Court of Judicature for the decision of differences between the several nations, although such Court [is] not to be armed with any coercive powers";[5] and (3) creation of a European "Congress or Diet" of representatives of each nation which would operate mainly by issuing "opinions" appealing to the force of public opinion.[6] After a certain time, the Diet could place the refractory State "under the ban of Europe."[7] Finally, in a passage neglected by most commentators: "There might, perhaps, be no harm in regulating, as a last resource, the contingent to be furnished by the several States for enforcing the decrees of the Court."[8] Thus, although somewhat hesitant about calling for an international police force to enforce decisions of the international tribunal, the essence of Bentham's proposal is clearly "world peace through enforceable law."

Although one American treatise writer insists upon finding Bentham's proposal to be "strikingly similar" to federalist proposals by Abbe de Saint Pierre (1712) and Rousseau (1761),[9] there is a critical difference: Bentham's "Diet" is not a world parliament that would make world law as part of a world government.[10] Rather, Bentham's proposal calls only for an institution of international dispute resolution, one of the first such proposals.[11] This is a huge difference since the prospects of adoption of Bentham's "world peace through law" proposal are almost literally infinitely greater than world federalism being adopted any time soon. It is clear, in short, that Bentham rejects both pacifism and world federalism, deliberately choosing his own more moderate and common-sense path, a path uncannily similar to our own twenty-first-century proposal, as will be seen.

There is an ongoing debate about what impact Bentham's plan had on the subsequent British (and world) peace movement.[12] In any event, it is clear that no popular "WPTL" movement developed. One can merely speculate as to several possible reasons. Perhaps, in view of the superficial similarity to the more dramatic proposals for world federalism, the fact that Bentham did not have his writings[13] published in his lifetime and the growth of pacifist and other peace societies as part of the generalized revulsion against war following the lengthy (1793–1815) Napoleonic Wars, Bentham's much more specific proposals were simply neglected.[14] Also, the fact that Bentham was viewed as being a tad eccentric may not have enhanced his credibility. In his will, he specified that Dr. Thomas Southwood Smith should dissect his body as part of a public anatomy lecture, that the preserved body be then clothed in one of his black suits and propped up in his favorite chair with a cane and placed in a glass-fronted case.[15] Said case and its contents were soon acquired by University College London[16] and it was put on public display in the South Cloisters wing of Main Hall, being wheeled in, it is said, for special board meetings with the ex officio board member being listed in the minutes as "present but not voting."

Notes

1 Bentham was an early proponent of, inter alia, freedom of expression, separation of church and state, equal rights for women, the right to divorce, the abolition of slavery, and decriminalization of homosexual acts.
2 Jeremy Bentham, Plan for an Universal and Perpetual Peace, at 12 (1789; Grotius Society Publ., 1927).
3 E.g., ever the humorist, he notes that even if England were successful in conquering France, why would they want to, even "Parliament itself…without paying it any very extraordinary compliment, would not wish it," such that even if they won "[y]ou would still be so much the worse, though it were to cost you nothing." Id. at 24. Bentham is not, however, a pacifist. See Stephen Conway, "Bentham, the Benthamites, and the Nineteenth-Century

British Peace Movement," 2 *Utilitas* 221 (1990) and note 8 infra (use of international force contemplated).

4 Forces, it may be noted, capable of "force projection," to use modern terminology. As will be seen, this part of his scheme tracks the first leg of our tripartite proposal, calling for abolition of the most offensive of modern weapons, nuclear weapons.

5 Id. at 26.

6 Id. at 30–31. Bentham gives as an example of the force of public opinion the instance where the citizens of Sweden objected to a war against Russia, with a considerable part of the army either refusing their commissions or refusing to act, with the result that the king had to retreat from the Russian frontier and call a Diet.

7 Id. at 31.

8 Id. Bentham adds that the need for such an international force would, "in all human probability," be obviated by the operation of a free press (guaranteed by the agreement establishing the Court) and public opinion. Id.

9 Henry Wheaton, History of the Law of Nations in Europe and America, at 343 (1845).

10 See Conway, supra, at 977: "Any attempt to vest the congress with powers that might lead to its becoming 'an Universal Republic' he considered inconsistent with national sovereignty." Similarly, Bentham's proposals could hardly have been borrowed from Immanuel Kant's later work on Perpetual Peace (1795) (calling for total abolition of national armies [not Bentham's proposal], a "federation of nations" [same], and an eventual "cosmopolitan constitution" [same]).

It is possible he got some ideas from Kant's philosophical musings in *Idea for a Universal History* (1784), but Kant here argues for "a distant international government" [again, not Bentham's proposal].

11 Remarkably, Bentham's proposal for international dispute resolution is not the first. That honor appears to belong to King George of Bohemia, who, in an almost completely forgotten detailed proposal of *1464* called for both an international organization similar to the subsequent League of Nations and the United Nations and some kind of international tribunal. See Jiri Z. Podebrad, The Universal Peace Organization of King George of Bohemia: A Fifteenth Century Plan for World Peace 1462/1464 (1972) (under Article 16 of a draft treaty, a so-called "Assembly" is given "voluntary and contentious jurisdiction with pure and mixed authority over all of us and our subjects as well as those who voluntarily submit thereto").

12 See Martin Ceadel, The Origins of War Prevention: The British Peace Movement and International Relations, 1730–1854, at 67–68, 194, 245–246, 291–292 (1996) (if nothing else, it is clear that Bentham contributed to the end of fatalism about war; also, on April 25, 1787, in a speech at the Meeting-house in the Old Jewry, London, he made "the earliest proposal for a peace association so far discovered"; he may have obtained the idea for a peace association from the 1787 Society for Effecting the Abolition of the Slave Trade; Bentham disciple adopts court tribunal idea in 1824; Bentham's 1789 essay not even published until 1843; influential British Peace Society in 1839 adopts Bentham-inspired proposal for "a high court of appeal, in which national disputes may be adjusted") and Conway,

supra, at 978–979 (although Bentham borrowed many ideas from others, his ideas were "seminal rather than derivative" and he acted as "a bridge connecting the Enlightenment with nineteenth-century liberalism").

13 An estimated 5 million words stored in 80 wooden boxes, of which this portion was a mere 44 pages in its current pamphlet form.

14 Cf. Joseph Preston Baratta, The Politics of World Federation: United Nations, UN Reform, Atomic Control, vol. 1, at 32 (2004) (Bentham's ideas "no match for the challenge of the Napoleonic wars that soon engulfed Europe").

15 Actually, this request was not just a sign of eccentricity. Ever the reformer, this unusual request was an effort to avoid the problem of hospitals and medical schools having no access to corpses for autopsies. Bentham felt his unusual bequest might lead to efforts to legalize the use of corpses for medical dissection classes.

16 Bentham was a co-founder of the college, which was open to Non-Conformists and Jews. Wikipedia at note 20.

4 Roosevelt and Taft (1910–1918)

Theodore Roosevelt[1]

One would never suspect that Theodore Roosevelt, an avid imperialist and trigger-happy former Assistant Secretary of the Navy, would be a proponent of World Peace Through Law, but he was.

Theodore Roosevelt received the Nobel Peace Prize for his efforts in mediating an end to the Russo-Japanese War in 1905. In his May 5, 1910, acceptance speech he spoke in his typical self-confident manner as a "practical man" who felt he had "the right to have my words taken seriously when I point out where, in my judgment, great advance can be made in the cause of international peace." He identified three areas for improvement:

(1) "treaties of arbitration" covering "almost all questions liable to arise between ... nations,"[2] which "until we have gone much further than at present in securing some kind of international police action," would "go a long way towards creating a world opinion which would finally find expression in the provision of methods to forbid or punish any violation"; (2) "further development of the Hague Tribunal [and] conferences"[3] so that arbitration could be "render[ed] ... effective" and a true "world court" created along the lines of the U.S. Supreme Court with similar effectiveness except "on a world scale"; and (3) "some kind of international police power" to "enforce the decrees of the court."

The supreme difficulty in connection with developing the peace work of The Hague arises from the lack of any executive power, of any police power to enforce the decrees of the court. In any community of any size the authority of the courts rests upon actual or potential force, on the existence of a police, or on the knowledge that the able-bodied men of the country are both ready and willing to see that the decrees of judicial and legislative bodies are put into effect. In new and wild communities where there is violence, an honest man must protect himself, and until other means of securing his safety are devised, it is both foolish and wicked to persuade him to surrender his arms while the men who are dangerous to the community retain theirs. He should not renounce the right to protect himself by his own efforts until the community is so organized that it can effectively relieve the individual of the duty of putting down violence. So it is with nations. Each nation must keep well prepared to defend itself until the establishment of some form of international police power, competent and willing to prevent violence as between nations. As things are now, such power to command peace throughout the world could best be assured by some combination between those great nations which sincerely desire peace and have no thought themselves of committing aggressions. The combination might at first be only to secure peace within certain definite limits and on certain definite conditions; but the ruler or statesman who should bring about such a combination would have earned his place in history for all time and his title to the gratitude of all mankind.[4]

This version of "world peace through law" is not the product of mere academic speculation, but rather the considered opinion of a very "practical" man who knew first-hand what war could do and knew that something very decisive and efficacious needed to be done about it.[5] He was, after all, intimately familiar with the workings of police enforcement from his years (1895 to 1897) as a New York City Police Commissioner.

In sum, while almost none of his biographers has chosen to give any emphasis to this historic Nobel Peace Prize speech,[6] and while its significance could easily have been lost amongst his many bellicose statements over the years,[7] this little-noticed 1910 speech is a long-lost milestone in humanity's quest for a lasting peace.[8]

William Howard Taft

Another prominent proponent of "world peace through law" is William Howard Taft, our 27th President (1909–1913), our 10th U.S. Supreme Court Chief Justice (1921–1930), our 42nd Secretary of War under Teddy Roosevelt (1904–1908) and our 5th Solicitor General (1890–1892). In short, very much the Establishment Man, and a Republican, in the days when it was still possible for Republicans to support anti-trust, the Interstate Commerce Commission, a federal income tax, and direct election of senators.

Most Americans would undoubtedly be surprised to learn that a Republican president was active in the peace movement. But as pointed out in an article by Harvard Law Professor David Kennedy:

> Prior to the outbreak of war [WWI], the American peace movement was dominated by prominent establishment jurists and industrialists such as Elihu Root [Secretary of War under McKinley and TR, TR's Secretary of State; first president Carnegie Endowment; Nobel Peace Prize, 1912), James Brown Scott [law dean and expert on international law; delegate to Second Hague Peace Conference; Secretary, Carnegie Endowment], William Howard Taft, Theodore Marburg [Taft protégé; Ambassador to Belgium], and Andrew Carnegie, who focused their attention on the Hague Conferences and the concomitant growth of public international law and arbitration ... Unlike the pacifists and social reformers, their early plans emphasized world peace under law rather than political reform.[9]

In an early (1914) speech Taft spelled out his belief in the efficacy of international arbitration:

> The ideal that I would aim at is an arbitral court in which any nation could make complaint against any other nation, and if the complaint is found by the court to be within its jurisdiction, the nation complained of should be summoned, the issue framed by pleadings, and the matter disposed of by judgment.[10]

This future Chief Justice (and, before that, professor of international law at Yale, and, first job out of law school, a former prosecutor) knows how the legal system works and sees no reason why it ought not to work analogously at the international level. He continues:

> It would, perhaps, sometimes require an international police force to carry out the judgment, but the public opinion would [itself] accomplish much.[11]

Later, in this same vein:

> But the query is made: "How will judgments of such a court be enforced; what will be the sanction for their execution?" I am very little concerned about that. After we have gotten the cases into court and decided and the judgments embodied in a solemn

declaration of a court, ...few nations will care to face the condemnation of international public opinion and disobey the judgment. When a judgment of that court is defied, it will be time enough to devise methods to prevent the recurrence of such an international breach of faith.[12]

Finally, he concludes:

> With such a system, we could count on a gradual abolishment of armaments and a feeling of the same kind of security that the United States and Canada have today which makes armaments and navies on our northern border entirely unnecessary.[13]

It is, in short, a fairly comprehensive and well-thought-out schema for world peace under law, although the commitment to an international peace force is a bit uncertain. In subsequent speeches he concedes that the "details are not worked out,"[14] and he backs off entirely from trying to enforce compliance on the ground that "we ought not to attempt too much."[15] Rather, it is contemplated that collective enforcement will be used "only to prevent the beginning of war before there has been a complete submission, hearing of evidence, argument, and decision or recommendation."[16] Taft has no problem with the idea of an international police force that would act in the same deterrent manner as local police,[17] but he is uneasy with envisioning an international police force to enforce judgments.

Under Taft's proposal, reliance is placed upon conciliation and arbitration as a prelude to judge-made law,[18] without ever needing to create a world legislative body.[19] Taft believes that international dispute resolution is sufficient and that "verily ... we are in sight of the Promised Land."[20]

Notes

1 For discussions of the pre-WWI American peace movement and proposals in particular for international arbitration, see generally, Mark W. Janis, American and the Law of Nations 1776–1939, Chapter 4 (2010) (an amazing history of multiple individuals and groups, e.g., Noah Worcester, whose 1814 book, A Solemn Review of the Custom of War, urged resort to an international "high court of equity" with compliance to be made "a point of national honor" and William Ladd, whose 1840 Essay on a Congress of Nations urged a world arbitral court); Shirley V. Scott, International Law, US Power: The United States' Quest for Legal Security, Chapter 2 (2012) (Universal Peace Union meeting in 1866 has over 5,000 attendees favoring arbitration; numerous congressional resolutions 1870–1900

favor arbitration); Warren F. Kuehl, Seeking World Order: The United States and International Organizations to 1920 (1969) (detailed history of "arbitrationists," "sanctionists" [believers in an international peace force], world federalists, and pacifists); and Merle Curti, Peace or War: The American Struggle 1636–1936 (1936) (numerous arbitration conferences, including NY Peace Society congress attended by 10 mayors, 19 congressmen, 4 supreme court justices, 2 presidential candidates, 40 bishops, and 27 millionaires; presidents favoring arbitration include Grant, Hayes, Garfield, Arthur, and McKinley).

2 He excepts out what he viewed (erroneously) as "the very rare cases where the nation's honor is vitally concerned." Cf. Peter Gay, The Cultivation of Hatred, at 65 (1993) (TR critical of "universal arbitration" idealists in a letter of 1907).

3 The Permanent Court of Arbitration was created at The Hague Conference of 1899. In 1902, President Roosevelt initiated the first use of the Court on an old claim with Mexico. The Second Hague Convention (1907) was first proposed by TR, though officially convened by Czar Nicholas II. A third convention proposed for 1915 was never held due to WWI. See David S. Patterson, Toward a Warless World: The Travail of the American Peace Movement 1877–1914, at 116 (1976).

4 www.nobelprize.org/nobel_prizes/peace/laureates/1906/roosevelt-lecture. html (noting sources, including New York Times, May 6, 1910, and The Works of Theodore Roosevelt, Vol. 18).

5 On August 5, 1906, TR wrote to Andrew Carnegie: "I hope to see real progress made at the next Hague Conference. If it is possible in some way to bring about a stop, complete or partial, to the race in adding to armaments, I shall be glad; but I do not yet see my way clear as regards the details of such a plan. We must always remember that it would be a fatal thing for the great free peoples to reduce themselves to impotence and leave the despotisms and barbarians armed. It would be safe to do so if there were some international police; but there is now no such system." The Theodore Roosevelt Web Book (entry for "Hague Conferences"), www.theodoreroosevelt.org/tr%20web%20book/TR_CD_to_HTML255. html. Similarly, he wrote to Sir Edward Grey (British Foreign Secretary) on February 1, 1915: "I agree absolutely with you that no treaty of the kind [Hague] should hereafter ever be made unless the Powers signing it bind themselves to uphold its terms by force if necessary." Id. (entry for "Hague Treaties").

6 The lone exception, out of nine, being Edmund Morris, Colonel Roosevelt, at 49–50, 137 (2010) (brief reference).

7 Cf. generally, James Bradley, The Imperial Cruise: A Secret History of Empire and War (2009). Cf. id. at 204: TR a proponent of use of U.S. military as an "international force" to enforce American foreign policy in Latin America.

8 It probably matters not whether some of the ideas may have come from Andrew Carnegie. But cf. David Nasaw, Andrew Carnegie, at 679, 683 (2006) (correspondence between TR and AC shows that TR originated the idea for "some system of international police," which AC then adopted). Of course, international arbitration was not a new idea, being, in fact, part of the Republican party platform in 1884.

9 David Kennedy, "The Move to Institutions," 8 *Cardozo L. Rev.* 841, 879–880 (1987) (emphasis added).
10 David H. Burton, ed., The Collected Works of William Howard Taft, vol. 6, at 182 (2003).
11 Id.
12 Id. at 200.
13 Id. at 182.
14 Collected Works, supra, vol. 7, at 65 (address of July 3, 1916).
15 Id. at 53 (address of June 17, 1915). He continues: "We believe that the forced submission, the truce taken to investigate and the judicial decision, or the conciliatory compromise recommended, will form a material inducement to peace. It will cool the heat of passion and will give the men of peace in each nation time to still the jingoes."
16 Id. at 65. See also World Peace: A Written Debate between William Howard Taft and William Jennings Bryan, at 22 (1917) (international peace force designed merely to "hold off members ... from war until the cooling and curative influence of the League's judicial procedure may have time to operate.").
17 See World Peace: A Written Debate, supra, at 22: "No matter how law-abiding a community, neither the statutes nor judgments of the Courts enforce themselves so as to dispense with police or sheriffs." Cf. id. at 34: "If we need fear of restraint to keep men in paths of peace and law, why not nations?"
18 Collected Works, vol. 6 at 200: "It will be judge-made law, and the growth of the international law will be as the common law has grown, adapting itself to new conditions and expanding on principles of morality and general equity." See John E. Noyes, "William Howard Taft and the Taft Arbitration Treaties," 56 *Vill. L. Rev.* 535, 543–548 (2011) (broad equity jurisdiction proposed, with no exception for questions of "national honor").
19 Collected Works, vol. 6 at 200: "It is, therefore, federation to the extent of a permanent international court that offers the solution to the problems of how to escape war, how to induce nations to give up the burden of armaments, and how to broaden and make certain our system of international law."
20 Collected Works, vol. 7 at 135 (speech at University of Wisconsin, November 9, 1918).

5 Kelsen (1944)

Hans Kelsen (1881–1973) was an Austrian jurist and legal philosopher who has been described as "possibly the most influential jurisprudent of the twentieth century."[1] Although much of his work dealt with general legal philosophy, in 1944 he authored a small book called "Peace Through Law."

Building upon an earlier work done at Harvard Law School, where he had been "taken up" by Dean Roscoe Pound,[2] he dealt directly and in plain language (unlike some of his recondite jurisprudential work) with the need to prevent another world war. He starts by noting all the work done on the peace issue by his predecessors:

> It would be unjust to ignore the many efforts which so far have been made by statesmen and intellectuals aiming at the idea of world peace. We must, however, admit that all these efforts have been in vain, that, in spite of them, social history in this respect, shows regress rather than progress. This may be because the statesmen almost always have ventured too little and the intellectuals have frequently demanded too much. The League of Nations was certainly too little; the dream of a World State is certainly too much.[3]

Kelsen believes that even a "simple writer" has a duty equal to that of the active statesman in the struggle for world peace, in language that speaks directly to current peace activists of all kinds (but most especially to world federalists):

> He must, in order not to compromise the great ideal, accommodate his postulates to what is politically possible ... A conscientious writer must direct his suggestions to what, after careful examination of political reality, may be considered as being possible tomorrow, although it, perhaps, seems not yet possible today.[4]

Further, since it is the Law of Nations which now regulates relations between States, "[h]e who wishes to approach the aims of world peace in a realistic way must take this problem quite soberly, as one of a slow and steady perfection of the international legal order."[5]

Kelsen starts by admitting that "the ideal solution" in theory to the problem of peace would be a World Federal State.[6] The only problem with this idea is that in the real world it is "confronted with serious and, at least at present, insurmountable difficulties."[7] A principal difficulty would be trying to organize such a World Federal State, since if it were done along democratic lines:

> a world parliament in which all the United Nations would be represented according to their aggregate numerical strength would be a legislative body in which India and China would have approximately three times as many deputies as the United States of American and Great Britain together.[8]

Moreover, the differences amongst peoples are simply too great, the effort to point to the examples of the United States and Switzerland being "a dangerous illusion."[9] Finally, Kelsen states that even if a world federation is possible in some very long run, "[f]rom a strategic point of view, there is but one serious question: What is the next step...?"[10]

For Kelsen the answer is clear. Since "international peace can be secured without the establishment of a World State," with the requisite "force monopoly" being "possible even if the centralization of the community does not reach the degree characteristic of a State,"[11] the "next step" is to establish "an international court endowed with compulsory jurisdiction,"[12] with enforcement of its orders and judgments by "an international police force...at the disposal of a central administrative agency whose function is to execute the decisions of the court."[13] He recognizes that there will be "stubborn resistance" to any such proposal from national governments[14] and that the organization of his proposed "administrative body" is undoubtedly "the most difficult of all the problems of world organization," something that would probably have to be accomplished gradually over time.[15]

The core of Kelsen's proposal is a functionalist and gradualist approach that (unlike most pacifists) recognizes a role for international force and (unlike the world federalists) rejects the need for a global legislature. He believes, rather, that international law will tend to develop and grow in much the same way as primitive pre-State law developed, via judicial institutions.[16] Thus:

> This settles another objection which is continually brought against the establishment of a compulsory international jurisdiction, namely, that the international legal order to be applied by the court is deficient and that international jurisdiction is not possible without an international legislative body competent to adapt international law to the changing circumstances. From the fact that it is impossible to form such a legislative body it is concluded that a compulsory international jurisdiction is also impossible.
>
> This argument is incorrect in every respect. As pointed out, the development of national law indicates on the contrary that the obligation to submit to the decision of the courts long precedes legislation, the conscious creation of law by a central organ. Within the individual State, courts have for centuries applied a legal order which could not be changed by any legislator, but which developed, exactly like present-day international law, out of custom and agreements; and in this legal system custom was for the most part formed by the practice of the courts themselves. An international court which exercises the jurisdiction of deciding all the legal disputes of those parties subject to the law, even if it is empowered by the constitution to apply only the positive law, gradually and imperceptibly will adapt this law in its concrete decisions to actual needs.[17]

As to the claim that most of the claims between nations that lead to conflict are economic or political in nature and therefore not "justiciable," i.e., resolvable on the basis of "law," Kelsen rejects the purported distinction outright, concluding that the fact that a dispute is economic or political "does not exclude treating the dispute as a legal dispute."[18]

Kelsen points out that his hope that all nations will consent to submit all their disputes without exception to the compulsory jurisdiction of an international court had the support of Prime Minister Winston Churchill in a speech he had made arguing for the old League of Nations:

> This hope has been supported by the above-mentioned speech of Prime Minister Churchill. He said that we must try to make the international organization to be established after this war "into a really effective League with all the strongest forces concerned

woven into its texture, with a high court to adjust disputes and with forces, armed forces, national or international or both, held ready to enforce these decisions and prevent renewed aggression and preparation for future wars."[19]

In sum, Hans Kelsen's version of "world peace through law" is a good deal more comprehensive than that of either Theodore Roosevelt (which exempted issues of "national honor") or President Taft (which was limited to "justiciable" questions). His more advanced and academically rigorous ideas have received, however, almost no attention from American political science and international relations and international law scholars.[20] The reason for this, it is submitted, is that the ghost of Hans Morgenthau walks the halls of American academia to this day.[21] And this dose of "political realism," it may be added, was almost certainly a necessary antidote to the overpromises of the pacifists and world federalists. Unfortunately, the upshot is that, at least in this country, Kelsen's moderate views have been largely neglected in battles between the more extreme positions.

Notes

1 David M. Walker, The Oxford Companion to Law, at 699 (1980). Cf. Roscoe Pound, "Law and the Science of Law in Recent Theories," 43 *Yale L.J.* 525, 532 (1934) (Kelsen "undoubtedly the leading jurist of the time"). But compare D.A. Jeremy Telman, "The Reception of Hans Kelsen's Theory in the United States: A Sociological Model," 24 L'Observatuer des Nations Unies 299 (2008) (Kelsen practically unknown in North America and American jurisprudence has totally ignored his contribution; America's most widely cited legal theorist, Judge Richard Posner, admits that until recently he had never read Kelsen) with Alexander Somek, "Kelsen Lives," 18 *European J. Int'l L.* 409 (2007). Cf. generally David Kennedy, "The International Style in Postwar Law and Policy," 1994 *Utah L. Rev.* 7 (1994).
2 Although Kelsen was legal advisor to the War Minister of Austria during WWI and was entrusted with drafting the new Austrian Constitution in 1920, he was dismissed from the Austrian Constitutional Court in 1930 for political reasons and dismissed from a law professorship at the University of Cologne when the Nazis seized power in 1933. He left for Geneva, where he taught at the Graduate Institute of International Studies (1934–1940), developing an interest in international law. Because of fear that Switzerland might not be allowed to remain neutral, he fled to the USA, giving the Oliver Wendell Holmes Lectures at Harvard Law School in 1943.
3 Peace through Law, at viii.
4 Id. at viii–ix (emphasis added).
5 Id. at ix.

6 Id. at 5. The famous real-politiker Hans Morgenthau made a similar concession, much cited by world federalists: "The argument of the advocates of the world state is unanswerable: there can be no permanent international peace without a state coextensive with the confines of the political world." Hans J. Morgenthau, Politics among Nations, at 477 (1948). What they fail to cite is what he says next: "No society exists coextensive with the presumed range of a world state" and "the peoples of the world are not willing to accept world government." Id. at 478–479.

7 Peace through Law, at 5.

8 Id. at 10.

9 Id. at 12.

10 Id.

11 Id. at 9.

12 Id. at 14.

13 Id. at 19.

14 Id. Kelsen notes that it would be essential that Russia be part of this system. Id. at 15. Cf. Chapter 9 infra at note 55 (Gorbachev prepared to accept compulsory jurisdiction of International Court of Justice).

15 Id. at 20 (also noting that resolutions of this administrative council "need not require unanimity").

16 Id. at 22: "Natural evolution tends first toward international judiciary, and not toward international government or legislation."

17 Id. at 22–23.

18 Id. at 24. Cf. id. at 29: "A positive legal order can always be applied to any conflict whatever."

19 Id. at 57.

20 See Telman, supra. Cf. also David Kennedy, "The International Style in Postwar Law and Policy," 1994 Utah L. Rev. 7 (1994) (thoughtful analysis of Kelsen's "surprisingly modern" 1941 Holmes Lectures, undertaken despite fact that most international scholars, including his own dean, viewed Kelsen as "a leftover European philosophizer" not worth discussing) and Judith von Schmadel, "Kelsen's Peace through Law and Its Reception by his Contemporaries," 39 *Hitotsubashi J. of Law & Politics* 71, 82 (2011) ("the idea of peace through law has never really been forgotten," and in recent years Kelsen's ideas are receiving "renewed attention" [citing six European journals]).

21 See Shirley V. Scott and Radhika Withana, "The Relevance of International Law for Foreign Policy Decision-making When National Security Is at Stake: Lessons from the Cuban Missile Crisis," 3 *Chinese JIL* 163-168-169 (2004) (realism the "dominant paradigm in the study of International Relations since World War Two," led by Morgenthau).

6   Eisenhower and
Kennedy (1961)

Law day USA, 1958

Charles S. Rhyne (1912–2003) was a Special Counsel to President Eisenhower and proposed that he establish May 1st as Law Day USA.[1] Eisenhower liked the idea and assigned his speechwriter, Executive Assistant Arthur Larson, to draft a speech for a May 1, 1958, Law Day Proclamation. Larson, the former Dean of the University of Pittsburgh Law School, researched the topic of world peace under law, reading several books suggested by Charles Rhyne.[2] Although a major theme of the Law Day speech was a comparison of America's freedoms under the law with the Soviet Union's militaristic May Day exercises, the heart of this first Law Day speech was this passage: "In a very real sense, the world no longer has a choice between force and law. If civilization is to survive, it must choose the rule of law."[3]

Eisenhower subsequently questioned Larson about what the general concept of "world peace through law" would mean "in concrete terms."[4] Larson was ready with a prepared answer, saying it would require four things: (1) modernizing rules of international law; (2) appropriate dispute-settling machinery; (3) improved methods of compliance; and (4) acceptance by the world community.[5] Still later, Eisenhower expressed strong support for Larson's idea of establishing a World Rule of Law Research Center at Duke University and even expressed the view that it was a topic on which he would enjoy spending the rest of his life working if he had the time.[6] Shortly thereafter, however, the furor over the so-called "Bricker Amendment" eliminated any further discussion of the world rule of law idea. According to Larson, it "got lost in the shuffle."[7]

Nevertheless, Eisenhower maintained his interest in the "world peace through law" concept, an interest that he had expressed publicly before being elected president. On March 23, 1950, while President of

Columbia University, Ike spoke on "World Peace—A Balance Sheet."[8] General Eisenhower declared that "the world must finally disarm or suffer catastrophic consequences."[9] As to how this might be accomplished, he stated that a permanent peace is impossible "unless all [nations] are committed to disarmament, and there is some means of enforcing peace among them."[10] In this respect, he looked to some international "police power universally recognized and strong enough to earn universal respect."[11]

> How this [international peace] organization is to be constituted or how it is to be controlled, has yet to be worked out, but with principles honestly accepted, the procedural problems would be easy of solution.[12]

While he realized that "[p]rogress is bound to come from slow, evolutionary processes," it was important not to fall prey to pessimism and defeatism.[13]

Subsequently, in a speech before a joint session of Parliament in New Delhi, India, December 10, 1959, he said:

> The time has come for mankind to make the rule of law in international affairs as normal as it is now in domestic affairs. Of course, the structure of law must be patiently built, stone by stone ...
>
> Plainly one foundation stone of this structure is the International Court of Justice ... It is better to lose a point now and then in an international tribunal, and gain a world in which everyone lives at peace under a rule of law.[14]

The fact that Eisenhower "actually considered and even threatened using nuclear weapons more than any other president"[15] only reinforces the significance of his support of WPTL proposals. One could not ask for a more credible proponent of WPTL. But his views in this respect remain largely unknown to the American public.

John F. Kennedy's views

John F. Kennedy, in his short presidency, gave two speeches of historic significance relating to the peace issue. In his inaugural address of January 20, 1961, he stated the following:

> So let us begin anew ... Let both sides, for the first time, formulate serious and precise proposals for the inspection of arms—and

bring the absolute power to destroy other nations under the absolute control of all nations ... And let both sides join in creating a new endeavor, not a new balance of power, but a new world of law, where the strong are just and the weak secure and the peace preserved. All this will not be finished ... in the life of this Administration, nor even perhaps in our lifetime ... But let us begin.[16]

And on June 10, 1963, in a commencement address at American University:

What kind of peace to we seek? ... not merely peace in our time but peace for all time ... Let us examine our attitude toward peace itself. Too many of us think it is impossible. Too many think it unreal. But that is a dangerous, defeatist belief. It leads to the conclusion that war is inevitable—that mankind is doomed—that we are gripped by forces we cannot control. We need not accept that view Our problems are manmade—therefore, "they can be solved by man." ... World peace, like community peace, does not require that each man love his neighbor—it requires only that they live together in mutual tolerance, submitting their disputes to a just and peaceful settlement ... [W]e seek to strengthen the United Nations, ... to develop it into a genuine world security system—a system capable of resolving disputes on the basis of law ...[17]

The 1961 McCloy-Zorin agreement

Conceived under the Eisenhower and Kennedy administrations, the September 1961 McCloy-Zorin "Joint Statement of Agreed Principles for Disarmament Negotiations"[18] was a dramatic and far-reaching proposal for "general and complete disarmament in a peaceful world." The opening paragraphs of the Agreement state that such disarmament is to be accomplished "by the establishment of reliable procedures for the peaceful settlement of disputes and effective arrangements for the maintenance of peace," including "a United Nations peace force" that would have a monopoly of all internationally-useable military force. This is another variant of world peace through law.

Despite the obvious importance of this document, which admittedly was not ultimately adopted, this vital agreement is almost never mentioned by the current generation of international relations or international law scholars.[19] In 1986 I taught a Law and Contemporary Problems seminar on what I called "Law and World Peace." One of the students, Dick Samson, did a paper for the seminar titled: "The McCloy-Zorin Agreement: The Reflections of Mr. John J. McCloy."

On April 23, 1986, Mr. Sansom interviewed Mr. McCloy, then 91 years old, seeking to find out more about the McCloy-Zorin Agreement.

Mr. McCloy indicated that the administration had had contentious internal debates concerning how to respond to Soviet Premier Nikita Khrushchev's call for general and complete disarmament at the UN in 1959.[20] In an attempt to resolve the issue, President Eisenhower had appointed a group of individuals, including Mr. McCloy,[21] to delineate the parameters of any disarmament agreement. After attempting to do so, the group decided that they needed to have an open dialogue with the Soviets to ascertain how far they had gone in their thinking and "to determine whether or not these overtures were in fact sincere, or if they were simply more Soviet propaganda."[22]

McCloy was chosen to initiate this dialogue. Appointed by President Kennedy to head up the new Arms Control and Disarmament Agency, McCloy (1895–1989) was the ultimate Washington insider, a liberal Republican with superb establishment credentials as a successful Harvard-trained New York City lawyer, Assistant Secretary of War (1941–1945)[23], President of the World Bank (1947–1949), Military Governor and High Commissioner for Germany (1949–1952), Chairman of Chase Manhattan Bank (1953–1960), Chairman of the Ford Foundation (1958–1965)[24], Chairman of the influential Council on Foreign Relations (1954–1970), and presidential advisor of every president from FDR to Ronald Reagan.[25] His selection was "a clear signal" to the Soviets that the United States was taking this negotiation seriously.[26]

McCloy personally contacted Valerian Zorin, who was Deputy Minister of Foreign Affairs, to arrange a private meeting to discuss disarmament. McCloy vividly remembered their first meeting, with a distinct recollection of the initial discussion:

Q: (by McCloy)—Has your country given serious thought as to how far you are willing to go in order to reach a disarmament agreement with the United States?

A: (by Zorin)—Yes, we've gone far …

Q: (McCloy)—We have also been working hard at arriving at some type of decision regarding how far we would be willing to go. However, we presently are stopped in this process, and are hoping that by discussing our thoughts with you, we can (receive feedback) and get a feel for a common ground. Just how far have you gone? Do you have something in writing?

A: (Zorin)—Our government has given much thought to this (issue). We have been involved in discussions and have done some writing. We have given a great deal of thought to our position.

Q: (McCloy)—It seems as though you have given this as much, if not
more thought, than we have...

A: (Zorin)—We have had many discussions and written on the issue.
Our greatest concern is that we not make a judgment that is
contrary to our vital interest ...[27]

Future meetings followed in Washington, D.C. (June 19–30), Moscow
(July 17–29), and New York City (September 6–19). McCloy remembered the meetings as "long and arduous," with much argument and
setting forth of "must conditions" by both sides.[28] In particular, the
Soviet Union insisted on their long-standing formula of "general and
complete disarmament." McCloy confided to Mr. Samson that his administration team had had disagreements amongst themselves on this
very issue. The United States insisted that adequate inspection and
verification were essential.[29] Eventually, an agreement was reached.[30]
In McCloy's opinion:

> These negotiations represented a good faith effort on the part of
> both nations to abandon propaganda by attempting to call each
> other's bluffs and truly search for a viable agreement.[31]

Although the McCloy-Zorin Joint Statement is "a remarkable step
forward in international relations,"[32] it ultimately failed. As to why,
former Nuremberg Prosecutor Benjamin Ferencz opines:

> [T]he solemn declarations failed to be implemented because nei-
> ther power was able to move decisively away from its traditional
> concepts of unfettered national security based on military power.
> Fear and suspicion remained in control. The Soviets were ready
> to have their destruction of existing arms verified by international
> inspectors but they were not ready to allow anyone to check their
> existing stockpiles.[33]

McCloy himself stated that:

> "His [Khrushchev's] response was so emphatic that I knew it [the
> Agreement] would never work." Khrushchev was primarily opposed
> to the plan because of his personal lack of control over an interna-
> tional organization which was called for in the agreement to over-
> see the disarmament process ... Mr. McCloy quoted Khrushchev
> as essentially stating at one point, "I would have to have my head
> examined if I were ready to submit such a vital interest of the Soviets

to international arbitration over which we would have no control." Mr. McCloy recalled the issue of having no control had caused some concern among members of this country's group as well … Because Khrushchev's rejection was so emphatic, the United States decided not to attempt further negotiations at that time.[34]

That was in 1961. But in 1986, John J. McCloy told Dick Samson:

I sense a present urgency on the part of the Soviets under Gorbachev, to reach an accord with the United States on arms control. It would be wise on our part to once again make the attempt and try to ascertain if such an agreement is possible with them.[35]

Now decades later, nobody has yet made that attempt.[36]

Notes

1 Arthur Larson, Eisenhower: The President Nobody Knew, at 109 (1968). Rhyne was president of the American Bar Association and during his year in office (1957–1958) he made "peace through law" his main concern, creating the ABA Special Committee on World Peace Through Law, which held numerous worldwide conferences on the topic during the 1960s and early 1970s, attended by thousands, including numerous judges such as Chief Justice Earl Warren, heads of state, such as the king and queen of Greece, prominent lawyers, businessmen, and diplomats, such as Henry Luce and John J. McCloy. See Charles S. Rhyne, "The Athens Conference on World Peace Through Law," 58 *Am. J. Int'l. L.* 138–151 (1964) and William S. Thompson, "The Belgrade World Peace Through Law Conference," 57 *ABA J.* 1121 (1971) (1971 conference had over 4,000 attendees; resolution proposing world government defeated).
2 Larson, supra, at 109. Larson was a protégé of Eisenhower's, who was even encouraged by Eisenhower to think of running for president after his term. Larson had been an advocate for "Modern Republicanism" and his book with that theme, "A Republican Looks at His Party" (1956), was publicly endorsed by Ike. Considered the "chief theoretician" of the Eisenhower administration, his star fell when the Far Right attacked him and he left government to return to academia. See David L. Stebenne, Modern Republicanism: Arthur Larson and the Eisenhower Years, at x, 269 (2006). Cf. also Mike Wallace interview, September 14, 1958 (Larson referred to as the Administration's resident "egghead"), www.hrc.utexas.edu/multimedia/video/2008/wallace/larson_arthur.html.
3 Larson, supra, at 107.
4 Id. at 110.
5 Id.
6 Id. at 112.
7 Id. at 113. The "Bricker Amendment" is a series of proposed constitutional amendments made in the 1950's which would have restricted

presidential power to enter into treaties and executive agreements. Cf. David M. Golove, "Treaty-Making and the Nation: The Historical Foundations of the Nationalist Conception of the Treaty Power," 98 *Mich. L. Rev.* 1075, 1270–1278 (2000).

8 Peace with Justice: Selected Addresses of Dwight D. Eisenhower (1961).

9 Id. at 9.

10 Id. at 18.

11 Id.

12 Id. at 19.

13 Id. at 19–20.

14 Id. at 193–195 (emphasis added). Cf. id. at 223–224 (the goal is "to replace force with a rule of law among nations," and therefore he supports the compulsory jurisdiction of ICJ).

15 Stephen Sestanovich, "The Long History of Leading from Behind," *The Atlantic*, 94, 100 (January/February 2016).

16 www.5.bartleby.com/124/pres56.html (emphasis added).

17 www.presidency.ucsb.edu/ws/?pid=9266 (emphases added).

18 U.S.-USSR Report to the General Assembly, UN Doc. A/4879 (September 20, 1961), reprinted in Department of State Bulletin, vol. 45, no. 1163, pp. 589–590 (October 9, 1961), (endorsed by General Assembly, December 20, 1961).

19 See Allan McKnight & Keith Suter, The Forgotten Treaties: A Practical Plan for World Disarmament, at 30 (1983), ("the McCloy-Zorin principles, while still referred to occasionally, gradually faded into history and a new generation of disarmament activists came into being which had no knowledge of them.")

20 Samson, at 2 (May 5, 1986) (on file with author).

21 McCloy was Eisenhower's first choice to be Secretary of State but had been "vetoed" by Senator Robert Taft.

22 Samson, at 3–4 (quoting McCloy). Prior to this, the closest we had come to a disarmament agreement was in 1955, when "as soon as the Russians agreed to our own plan, we disagreed with our own plan." Fred J. Cook, The Warfare State, at 231 (1962).

23 McCloy was "one of a handful of War Department officials aware of the Manhattan Project … The bomb was always in the back of McCloy's mind." Kai Bird, The Chairman John J. McCloy: The Making of the American Establishment, at 185 (1992).

24 Where he was asked to chair a task force study on the problems of world peace. Kai Bird at 386.

25 Benjamin B. Ferencz, A Common Sense Guide to World Peace, at 29 (1985). See Bird at 460–467 (McCloy participated in early CFR study groups re US-Soviet relations and nuclear weapons) and 501–515 (McCloy already had crux of idea for eventual Accord in early 1961 [speech at Philips Andover; June memo to JFK], including need for "reliable procedures…for the just settlement of disputes," "international arbitration, the extension of the jurisdiction of the International Court, the application of international sanctions by impartial tribunals not subject to veto," many of these ideas coming from Grenville Clark).

26 Samson, at 4. Cf. Bird at 498 (JFK needed "a conservative to execute a liberal policy").

27 Id. at 5 (parentheses in the original).
28 Id. at 6.
29 Id.
30 The full text is available at www.napf.org.
31 Samson, at 7.
32 Ferencz, supra, at 30.
33 Id. at 30–31 (emphases in the original).
34 Samson, at 9.
35 Samson, at 10.
36 But cf. House Concurrent Resolution No. 36 (1985) (an unsuccessful effort by Repr. George E. Brown, Jr. and 70 co-sponsors to call upon the President to re-initiate efforts to assess the viability of McCloy-Zorin approach). There is no evidence that the congressmen were aware that McCloy was still alive, or that he was aware of their proposed resolution.

7   Our trajectory

Despite the shameful years of the George W. Bush administration, years that are a testament to the perils of global illegalism,[1] we have not yet inflicted irreparable harm upon America's reputation, and our trajectory is even now toward a new world of peace and justice under the global rule of law.

What evidence is there for such starry-eyed optimism? There is ample evidence. If one takes a long view of our history as a species and as a gradually maturing global society, it becomes apparent that we are already building, brick-by-brick, law-by-law, and norm-by-norm, a growing body of what might be called "world-law-in-the-making"[2] right before our unsuspecting eyes.

One can start by merely charting a list of some of the highlights of international law[3] and institutions, built up primarily over only the past few centuries,[4] to remind ourselves of the progress that has been made, despite the many shortcomings that yet remain (Table 7.1).

What the above partial list makes clear is that—starting from the smallest measures, on up through the sweeping changes of the post-WWII years—a growing body of global law of considerable depth and breadth has gradually been accumulated. As stated recently in a text by some very "centrist" international law/international relations scholars, "[i]n many issue-areas, the world is witnessing a move to law."[5] To quote another very centrist international law professor:

> With the "globalization" of the world economy, and the externalization of matters that once were considered to be purely national, international law now applies to many subjects and fields of law—such as criminal law, environmental law, family law, the jurisdiction and judicial procedures of US courts, human rights, and economic, political and social activities of states in the United States—that previously were regulated mostly or even solely by domestic law.[6]

Increasingly also, international law is gradually procuring what the German legal philosopher Georg Jellinek called "praktische Geltung," practical validity.[7] This is happening at the very same time as recent sustained and strenuous attacks upon international law by neo-conservative critics.[8]

I do not intend to, nor do I need to, weigh in on the much-debated question of whether international law is real "law."[9] For present purposes, it is sufficient to make only a few simple points. First, while the neo-conservatives make some good points about the current inadequacy of international law, do they then go on to suggest how to correct and improve it? No, not once, because it is apparent that they have a hidden normative agenda, to weaken it.[10] Whether they will be successful remains to be seen. But for my part, I believe that their revisionist efforts risk a "descent into social chaos,"[11] a place we have been to and do not want to soon return.[12] By weakening international law, they are in the end obstructing one of humanity's "best means of creating a better world for all."[13]

Second, Eric Posner, perhaps the leading neo-conservative "revisionist," seems to argue that unless and until we have world government, the inadequacy of international law is inevitable,[14] which is not true. It is the central thesis of this book that there is an in-between position—short of world government yet more than "global legalism"—that can carry us past the nuclear age to a new and more stable form of global security. It is called "world peace through law," a topic he never addresses.

While it is true, in short, that current international law and institutions are weak and ineffective, especially in the critical area of global security,[15] they are growing stronger every day. To take one example in the area of international trade: Initially, the GATT (General Agreement on Tariffs and Trade, 1947) operated upon only a consensus decision-making basis. Now, however, since 1994 the new WTO (World Trade Organization) has precisely the reverse rule: sanctions are now automatic upon a finding by the WTO Tribunal in the absence of a consensus blocking them.[16]

Similarly, the Law of the Sea Treaty (1982) replaces a welter of conflicting power-based claims with a comprehensive rule-based framework to regulate all ocean space (70% of the globe), its uses and resources, from navigation rights to definition of territorial waters and related boundaries to fishing limits and other ocean resources regulation, all enforced via compulsory dispute settlement procedures.[17] Although the Law of the Sea Convention (UNCLOS) was the result of UN-sponsored conferences over many years, the UN now has no direct role in its operation, so that UNCLOS is free of the P-5 veto in the Security Council.[18]

These two examples of "stronger" international law are emblematic of the kinds of evolutionary changes that have taken place and will only continue to occur over time. And gradually the edifice of international law will become more and more impressive and gain greater acceptance. Much of this change will occur, not in the context of nations engaged in negotiating multilateral treaties but rather, increasingly, in day-to-day litigation in courtrooms all over the world where attorneys serving clients and judges hearing cases are inevitably forced to deal with issues of international law. Mr. Justice Stephen G. Breyer described this ongoing process in a speech on "International Governance and American Law" at the Brookings Institution on June 24, 2008:

> [S]ometimes I think of these lawyers across the world and the judges to a degree, as [being] like...bees. They're all out there building something. And you can't stop them, because their clients want and need the information, and there's no way to get it, without learning something about the law of other countries,[19] and then inevitably trying to put things together in a rational sensible way.
>
> That's the nature of the human mind. To impose a structure on this mess whether it is law or whether it is something else. But that's what we do. And we're doing it, and who brings it all together? Not me. I can just report that I'm part and you're part of an enterprise that's putting that kind of thing together, and that's changing the nature of law.
>
> Whether people argue about it in Congress, or don't. It is a fact that is continuing. And it's done on a level of people who are professional people. Not politicians ... But it's happening, it's going on and there's no way to stop it ...[20]

This ongoing process, which is gradually turning weak "international law" into enforceable and effective "world law," is very like the growth of the early common law. In twelfth and thirteenth-century Britain, with the centralization of justice following the Norman Conquest, the common law crimes and torts grew up one-by-one, gradually converting a hodgepodge of primitive local and feudal folkways reliant upon self-help remedies (the blood feud and its composition) into a systematic legal structure of Pleas of the Crown and civil causes of action enforceable in the central royal courts.[21] Similarly, various legal institutions, such as trial by jury and an independent parliament, only gradually came into existence, after continual struggles and even occasional battles, transforming what were arms of royal power and control into what we now view as democratic individual-freedom-enhancing legal institutions.[22] A similar evolutionary process is at work in the field of international law.

It is true, of course, that many of the more recent advances have not yet been signed by the United States.[23] This, despite the fact that many in the United States, such as Ambassador Eliot Richardson, chief U.S. negotiator at the Law of the Sea Conference during its critical phase, and Bill Pace, Convenor of the NGO Coalition for an International Criminal Court, played key roles in their creation. But this will change. America will eventually come around and play a part in this historic process.

In sum, despite the resistance of those fighting a fierce rearguard action, the move to international/world law is quite clear.

Table 7.1 Milestones in International Law

Hugo Grotius' *On the Law of War and Peace* (attempts to describe what he insists on calling "a common law of nations," albeit one that he freely admits is often as not observed in the breach)	1625
Peace of Westphalia (modern system of sovereign European states; early attempt at international arbitration)	1648
Final Act of Congress of Vienna (principles for cooperative use of rivers; etc.)	1815
Paris Declaration on Maritime Law (regulating maritime warfare)	1856
International Red Cross	1864
International Telecommunications Union	1865
Alabama Claims arbitration	1872
Institut de Droit International founded (Ghent)	1873
Int'l Bureau of Weights & Measures & Int'l Meteorological Org.	1878
Int'l Copyright Union	1886
First Hague Convention (against poison gas, dumdum bullets; treatment of war prisoners)	1899
Permanent Court of Arbitration	1900
Second Hague Convention (outlaws war to collect debt; accepts "principle" of compulsory arbitration, but without operative machinery)	1907
International Labor Organization	1919
International Civil Aviation Organization	1919
League of Nations [but not the U.S.]	1920
World Court [later, Int'l Court of Justice (1945)]	1921
Kellogg-Briand Pact (normative principle outlawing war, but no enforcement mechanism)	1928
Geneva Conventions on Prisoners of War	1929
Bank for International Settlements	1930
UNESCO	1942

(Continued)

World Bank	1944
IMF	1944
United Nations	1945
FAO (food & agriculture)	1945
Nuremberg War Crimes Trials begin	1945
UNICEF	1946
GATT (General Agreement on Tariffs & Trade)	1947
Universal Declaration of Human Rights	1948
World Health Organization	1948
Genocide Convention	1948
Geneva Convention on War Crimes	1949
European Coal & Steel Community	1951
European Convention for Protection of Human Rights	1953
European Economic Community (Treaty of Rome)	1957
IAEA (International Atomic Energy Agency)	1957
OECD (Organization for Economic Cooperation & Development)	1961
McCloy-Zorin Agreement (draft plan for nuclear disarmament)	1961
Limited Test Ban Treaty	1963
World Food Program	1963
UNCTAD (integrating developing countries into world economy)	1964
UNDP (development)	1965
Outer Space Treaty	1967
Treaty of Tlatelolco (first of several nuclear free zone treaties)	1967
Nuclear Nonproliferation Treaty	1968
Vienna Convention on the Law of Treaties	1969
Seabed Arms Control Treaty	1971
Biological Weapons Convention	1972
ABM Treaty [U.S. withdrew in 2001]	1972
SALT I Interim Agreement	1972
UNEP (environment)	1972
Threshold Test Ban Treaty	1974
Int'l Covenant on Economic, Social & Cultural Rights [but not U.S.]	1977
Convention on Elimination of Discrimination Against Women [id.]	1979
Law of the Sea Convention [id; entered force, 1994]	1982
Montreal Protocol (re ozone layer)	1987
Intermediate-Range Nuclear Forces Treaty	1987
Convention on the Rights of the Child [only U.S. & Somalia not]	1989
UN Framework Convention on Climate Change	1992
Chemical Weapons Convention	1993
Int'l Criminal Tribunal for the Former Yugoslavia	1993
WTO (more court-like sanctions than GATT)	1994
Comprehensive Test Ban Treaty [not approved by U.S. Senate]	1996
Ottawa Landmines Treaty [but not U.S.; entered force, 1999]	1997
Int'l Criminal Court [but not U.S.; entered force, 2002]	1998
UN Security Council "Responsibility to Protect" Resolution	2006
Convention on Cluster Munitions [but not U.S.; entered force, 2010]	2008
Paris Climate Change Agreement [but not U.S.]	2015

Notes

1 See generally, Philippe Sands, Lawless World: America and the Making and Breaking of Global Rules (2005); Nicole Deller, Arjun Makhijani, & John Burroughs, eds., Rule of Power or Rule of Law? An Assessment of U.S. Policies and Actions Regarding Security-Related Treaties (2003); Craig Eisendrath & Melvin A. Goodman, Bush League Diplomacy: How the Neoconservatives Are Putting the World at Risk (2004) and Berman, supra 84 Tex. L. Rev. at 1265 n. 2 (the administration's official National Defense Strategy goes so far as to lump the use of international "judicial processes" and terrorism as "strategies of the weak" that threaten "our strength as a nation state").

2 See Percy E. Corbett, The Growth of World Law, at 50 (1970) (we can regard the current international normative order as "a world legal system in the making"). Cf. also Neil Walker, Intimations of Global Law, at 145, 176 (2015) ("irreversible trend" toward global law, albeit "detailed trajectory is unclear").

3 According to scholarly researches, there are over 50,000 treaties, so we are being necessarily selective. Cf. O'Connell, supra, at 122.

4 This is not to say that there were not significant developments in international law prior to this. See, e.g., Harold Berman, "The Law of International Commercial Transactions (*Lex Mercatoria*)," 2 *Emory J. Int'l Disp. Resol.* 235 (1987) (tracing origins of law merchant from the Sea Law of Rhodes, ca. 300 BC). But with the evolution of the nation state in the early 1600s, see Sheri Berman, "From the Sun King to Karzai: Lessons for State Building in Afghanistan," 89 Foreign Affairs 2 (Mar/Apr 2010), we see the growth of international law. Cf. Mark W. Janis, "Jeremy Bentham and the Fashioning of 'International Law,'" 78 *Am. J. Int'l L.* 405 (1984) (Jeremy Bentham first to coin term "international law").

5 Judith L Goldstein, Miles Kahler, Robert O. Keohane, & Anne-Marie Slaughter, eds., Legalization and World Politics, at 4 (2001) (emphasis added).

6 John F. Murphy, The United States and the Rule of Law in International Affairs, at 6 (2004). Cf. Joel P. Trachtman, The Future of International Law, at 41, 74–84, 288–293 (2013) (likely future demographic and economic and technology changes will increase demand for international law and increase capacity for monitoring compliance).

7 Martii Koskenniemi, The Gentle Civilizer: The Rise and Fall of International Law 1870–1960, at 200 (2001). Cf. Thomas Pogge, "Moral Progress," Chapter 17 in Steven Luper-Foy, ed., Problems of International Justice, at 300 (1988) ("What I envision is the gradual establishment, one by one, of firm value-based institutional fixed points that stand above ordinary negotiation and bargaining and are immune to shifts in the power, interests, and opportunities of governments. Even institutions that once began as negotiated bargains could slowly and undramatically develop into such fixed points.").

8 See, e.g., Eric Posner, The Perils of Global Legalism, at 93 (2009) ("international law will become weaker over time"); Jack L. Goldsmith and Eric A. Posner, The Limits of International Law, at 199 (2005) ("we cannot condemn a state merely for violating international law"); Michael Stokes

Paulsen, "The Constitutional Power to Interpret International Law," 118 *Yale L.J.* 1762, 1786 (2009) ("The 'binding' international law character of a treaty obligation is, as a matter of U.S. law, largely illusory."); and Robert J. Delahanty & John C. Yoo, "Peace Through Law? The Failure of a Noble Experiment," 106 *Mich. L. Rev.* 923 (2008) (imply that because "collective security" failed in the two world wars, therefore "the idealistic goal of world peace through international law" failed; obviously fallacious reasoning, since of course WPTL has never been tried).

9 See, e.g., Anthony D'Amato, "Is International Law Really 'Law'?," 79 *NW U. L. Rev.* 1293 (1985) and Harold Hongju Koh, "Why Do Nations Obey International Law?," 106 *Yale L.J.* 2599 (1997). See also Michael P. Scharf, "International Law in Crisis: A Qualitative Empirical Contribution to the Compliance Debate," 31 *Cardozo L. Rev.* 45 (2009)(brilliant study proving that international law does make a difference; two proofs: (1) empirical study of ten living State Department Legal Advisers demonstrating that international law, in fact, made a difference in their decision-making; (2) demonstration that even the neo-cons themselves paid immense attention to international law in dealing with the controversial issues surrounding the treatment of detainees in the war on terror, to the point where they even purposely excluded then Legal Adviser William Howard Taft IV from their absurd memoranda for fear that he would disagree with their "Tea Party" versions of the law).

10 See Mary Ellen O'Connell, The Power and Purpose of International Law: Insights From the Theory and Practice of Enforcement, at 14 n. 59 (2008); Paul Schiff Berman, "Seeing Beyond the Limits of International Law," 84 Tex. L. Rev. 1265, 1279 (2006); and Oona Hathaway and Ariel N. Lavinbuk, "Rationalism and Revisionism in International Law," 119 *Harv. L. Rev.* 1404, 1427 (2006).

11 Thomas M. Franck, "The Power of Legitimacy and the Legitimacy of Power: International Law in an Age of Power Disequilibrium," 100 *Am. J. Int'l L.* 88, 92 (2006).

12 See R.J. Overy, Goering: Hitler's Iron Knight, at 229 (2003) (Goering considered treaties as "so much toilet paper.") and Isabel V. Hull, A Scrap of Paper: Breaking and Making International Law during the Great War (2014).

13 O'Connell, supra, at 15. The late Thomas Franck well understood the stakes here. He realized that what purports to be only "descriptive-empirical" can have "enormous prescriptive potential," such that what "spin" one puts on international law—positive vs. negative—can have serious consequences in the real world; "it is serious business." Franck, supra, 100 Am. J. Int'l Law at 90, 93.

14 Posner, The Perils of Global Legalism, at 7–12, 80–81, 128–129.

15 See Percy E. Corbett, The Growth of World Law, at 50 (1970) (the international legal system "leaves off precisely at the point where law is most necessary, namely where the urge to unrestrained action is strongest.").

16 See Richard H. Steinberg, "Judicial Lawmaking at the WTO: Discursive, Constitutional, and Political Constraints," 98 *Am. J. Int'l L.* 247 (2004); Bernhard Zangl, "Judicialization Matters! A Comparison of Dispute Settlement under GATT and the WTO," 52 *Int'l Studies Q.* 825 (2008) (also noting increased political independence of the Appellate Body and the use of legal reasoning instead of political bargaining); and Daniel Terris, Cesare P.R. Romano, & Leigh Swigart, The International

Judge: An Introduction to the Men and Women Who Decide the World's Cases, at 105–107 (2007), (inside story of how this process took place).

17 Cf. generally, Louis B. Sohn, Kristen G. Juras, John E. Noyes, & Erik Franckx, Law of the Sea in a Nutshell (2d ed. 2010).

18 This aspect of UNCLOS is of great interest. For this "Law of the Sea approach"—a functionalist approach keyed to a particular problem and neatly avoiding the constraints of the P-5 veto—could serve as a model for use in other areas (including the creation of WPTL). See Center for War/Peace Studies, "What Elliot Richardson Thinks," Global Report, at 1 (No. 4, 1978) (Amb. Richardson is interviewed by Richard Hudson, and states this: "To me the Law of the Sea Conference offers the hope of a major contribution in the building of a global order. It may well be the single most important potential to build it."

19 Justice Breyer explained that some 30 members of our illustrious Congress had introduced a bill that would have forbidden judges from ever referring to a foreign court opinion in their decisions! He had also noted that he had done a quick study and discovered that of 80 cases heard in one year, 9 raised serious questions of either international law or the law of some other nation. Transcript, at 2, 14. Cf. also Mark W. Janis, America and the Law of Nations 1776–1939, Chapters 1–4 (2010) (numerous cases from early 1800's also referred to foreign law and international law; early treatise writers in America, such as Kent and Story, also dealt with the law of nations).

20 Transcript, at 18 (emphases added). Cf. also Noah Feldman, "When Judges Make Foreign Policy," *New York Times*, at 50 (September 28, 2008) (noting that the Supreme Court "has no choice about whether to involve itself [in these questions] … it is now unavoidably involved.").

21 See generally, Harold Berman, Law and Revolution: The Formation of the Western Legal Tradition, Chapters 1–3, 13 (1983) and James T. Ranney, Heritage of Our Freedoms: Milestones in Legal History, at 16, 19–20 (1987), (slideshow transcript, on file with author).

22 See generally, Ranney, Heritage, at 20–21, 26–28 (also cf. "Milestones in Legal History" Appendix at 3–5 nn. 28, 31 & 39) (jury develops out of royal inquest of local knights of the shire [focusing on tax collection for the king] into independent criminal trial jury ca. 1220; subsequent development of right to freedom of deliberation established in 1670 case; parliament grows out of a body mainly "judicial" in nature or merely advisory to king into something approaching an independent legislature ca. 1258); Theodore F. Plucknett, A Concise History of the Common Law, at 118–121, 133–134 (5th ed. 1956); and J.R. Maddicott, The Origins of the English Parliament 924–1327 (2010).

23 There is an argument that these and similar treaties should have been adopted via the congressional-executive agreement process rather than via the treaty clause. See Oona Hathaway, "Treaties' End: The Past, Present, and Future of International Lawmaking in the United States," 117 *Yale L.J.* 1236 (2008) (former method obviously more democratic, and the two-thirds rule is based upon now-discredited concerns of the slaveholding states). Cf. generally, Glen S. Krutz & Jeffrey S. Peake, Treaty Politics and the Rise of Executive Agreements (2009). Cf. also Jessica T. Matthews, "The Death of Our Treaties," *New York Review of Books*, March 24, 2016, at 28–30 (U.S. risks losing role as world leader due to Senate's nearly automatic opposition to any new treaty).

8 Abolition of nuclear weapons

On November 20, 1985, at the Geneva Summit, President Ronald Reagan, and Soviet General Secretary Mikhail Gorbachev issued a historic joint statement that "a nuclear war cannot be won, and must never be fought."[1] A year later, at the October 1986 Reykjavik Summit, Reagan and Gorbachev followed up on their Geneva statement with dramatic proposals for the total abolition of nuclear weapons, which in the end foundered upon Reagan's commitment to so-called missile defense.

Although Reagan was immediately criticized by "nuclear realists" such as Senator Sam Nunn and former Secretary of State Henry Kissinger for proposing abolition, 20 years later Nunn and Kissinger joined former Secretary of Defense William Perry and former Secretary of State George Shultz in adopting Reagan's ideas.

The Four Horsemen of the Non-Apocalypse, in their justly famous Wall Street Journal editorial of January 4, 2007, called for "a world free of nuclear weapons." Having looked for decades at the various dead-ends to which nuclear weapons led, and the "increasingly hazardous" and "more precarious" nuclear future in which (a) even unpredictable third world tin-pot dictators were now fully capable of acquiring nuclear weapons, and (b) nuclear materials could more easily fall into the hands of undeterrable terrorists, the Gang of Four endorsed Reagan and Gorbachev's vision of a nuclear-free world.

Similarly, hundreds of retired military leaders and political leaders from all over the world have come out for abolition, and to name just a few: Admiral Noel Gaylor, Admiral Eugene Carroll, General Lee Butler, General Andrew Goodpaster, General Charles Horner, George Kennan, Melvin Laird, Robert McNamara, Colin Powell, and George H.W. Bush.[2] In short, the idea of abolishing nuclear weapons has moved from being the view of a prophetic few[3] to being the new consensus position,[4] held by approximately 80% of the American public.[5]

Despite this shift in both elite and public opinion, 20 years after the supposed end of the Cold War, we still have thousands of nuclear missiles ready to go off in minutes, with a collective force many thousands of times the power of the Hiroshima bomb.[6] With "a decision window for each country's president of four to eight minutes" (after deducting time for missile attack detection and confirmation, and the time for the response launch sequence and fly-away),[7] the increasingly decrepit Russian C-3 (command, control, communications) systems, and a long history (still largely unknown to the American public) of "near misses" with nuclear war,[8] it is no wonder that those in the know have become disenchanted with our current strategic posture. As one very knowledgeable nuclear weapons industry insider puts it: "It has always been acknowledged that an international security system based on the willingness of nations to commit mutual suicide in order to protect themselves is a suboptimum solution to the security dilemma."[9] Suboptimal indeed. George Shultz summed up the situation as concisely as anyone when confronted by the neo-conservatives about what almost happened at Reykjavik, he replied: "What's so great about a world that can be blown up in 30 minutes?"[10]

In sum, we find ourselves in a deeply paradoxical situation where both candidates for president in 2008 ran on platforms of abolishing nuclear weapons, where we are already theoretically obligated to eliminate them pursuant to the 1968 Non-Proliferation Treaty (Article VI), and yet, for whatever reasons—bureaucratic inertia or the machinations of the military-industrial-congressional-academic-media complex—we have thousands of nuclear weapons still ready and waiting to more or less end the world in the course of one rather long afternoon.[11]

Despite all of the above, there is a growing sense, a building momentum, a feeling that now is finally the time for abolition. Two basic arguments are being made for abolition: (1) that nuclear weapons, on balance, do not add to our security, but detract from it (the strategic argument); and (2) that they are barbaric relics that have no proper place in military armories (the moral argument). Most emphasis has been placed upon the first of these arguments. What is involved is a rather complicated assessment of relative risks. Those who have looked longest and hardest at the paths where continued reliance upon nuclear weapons leads have, with surprising unanimity,[12] concluded that this is simply "too frightful and dangerous a way to live indefinitely."[13] As Robert McNamara (who was Manager of Our Missiles for longer than anybody) puts it: "The indefinite combination of human fallibility and nuclear weapons carries a very high risk of nuclear catastrophe."[14]

Many if not most of the recent books, however, while occasionally talking about the need to "de-legitimize" nuclear weapons, do not focus on the moral question.[15] It is almost as if they are so eager to avoid being characterized as somehow too "idealistic" and insufficiently "clear-eyed" and "hard-headed" as those strategic brainiacs of old who coolly calculated and contemplated world-wide gigadeaths (deaths in the billions) that they repeatedly miss opportunities to state the fairly obvious. That these are not "military" weapons; they are, as Ronald Reagan and Mikhail Gorbachev stated, "irrational and inhumane." They are "a vast structure of cruelty"[16] designed and carefully maintained at the ready to—within less than 20 minutes of launch—boil, fry, incinerate, evaporate, maim, and irradiate huge numbers of innocent human beings. Professor Philip Allott nicely captures the true enormity of their evil:

> In the 20th century, the crazy idea that the human race might not survive was treated as a suitable topic for rational discussion and rational decision-making. People who are otherwise sane and sensible could talk about Mutual Assured Destruction and the End of Civilisation. People who are otherwise sane and sensible could make and manage total war, wars with no necessary geographical limit, no effective limit to the methods of death and destruction, no limit to the suffering to be endured by powerless and blameless human beings. In the 20th century, people who are otherwise decent and caring could regard it as regrettable, but natural, that countless millions of human beings should live in conditions of life which are a permanent insult to their humanity.[17]

Indeed, it is not too much to say that nuclear weapons have had, and are having, a corrosive effect on our moral fiber and sensibilities. Not only do they create an underlying perpetual sense of fear, leading to nihilistic feelings of futility,[18] they also pervasively color all our thinking, whether we realize it or not.

The objections to abolition

Of the many possible objections to abolition, the following seem to be the leading ones.

You cannot disinvent nuclear weapons

This, is of course true, but it is no objection to abolition. You cannot "disinvent" chemical and biological weapons, but we did abolish them in the Biological Weapons Convention (1972) and the Chemical Weapons Convention (1993). Secondly, as Jonathan Schell first pointed out, the very fact that the nuclear genie is permanently out of the bottle is what will permit a sort of virtual nuclear deterrence to continue to work in a nuclear-free world, but without the actual weapons sitting there poised to go off in minutes. There remains a disquieting problem with this concept, however, which is that it is arguably inconsistent with the abolitionist/de-legitimization mission. Thus, while there may be some inevitable role for virtual deterrence, there is a growing consensus that we need to set our face determinedly against any ideas of reconstituting nuclear weapons. If we ever do need to confront a recalcitrant nuclear law breaker, conventional forces will easily suffice (as a last resort).[19]

Abolishing nuclear weapons would make the world "safe" for conventional war

This is probably the most serious objection to abolition.[20] But despite a certain surface plausibility, when one looks at it carefully, it gradually loses its force. For one thing, it is fair to ask, as Barry Blechman does:

> Has there been peace in Europe (Yugoslavia aside) for the past 60-plus years because Britain, France, and Russia have nuclear weapons, or because the national rivalries that led to the wars of the twentieth century have been replaced by a common understanding in that part of the world that the price of modern war, even with conventional weapons, is horrendous and that international cooperation and integration is by far the better course?[21]

Moreover, as pointed out by several scholars: (1) even in a world of zero nuclear weapons, Schell's "knowledge is deterrence" concept would be operative to some extent; (2) the United States has a huge edge over every other country in conventional weapons, and this would deter just as well as nuclear weapons;[22] (3) at bottom, a nuclear-weapon-free world would be much safer than one with such weapons; and (4) nuclear weapons are in the end sociopathic and immoral weapons which, like mustard gas or smallpox or the plague bacillus, have no place in a civilized world and can therefore no longer be tolerated.

"Breakout" possibility

Probably the most common objection to abolition is the possibility of "breakout."[23] But this objection is easily rebutted upon even cursory examination. It turns out that if you run various simulations on what a breakout state might accomplish with a few or even a great many nuclear warheads, "it would not be able to do much of anything with them at all."[24] Far from suddenly being able to "rule the world," as postulated by abolition objectors, they would be confronted with not only the United States' awesome conventional forces but the combined military might of the whole world.[25] Moreover, the worldwide moral outrage would condemn them as an international pariah, something that "nuclear realists" tend to discount, but something that in the real world tends to make quite a difference.[26]

Verification and enforcement concerns

It has been objected that a treaty abolishing nuclear weapons could not be satisfactorily verified. With each passing year, in which we gain new means of verification beyond national technical means— including radioisotope monitoring, portal and perimeter continuous monitoring, environmental sampling, wide area surveillance, real-time surveillance, on-site sensors, hydroacoustic and seismic and infrasound monitoring—this will not be a valid objection to an abolition regime. It is true that nothing less than a very intrusive and solid verification regimen will be necessary. It will take hard work, and it will be costly, but there is a broad consensus that it can be done.[27]

Next, as to the key issue of enforcement. In addition to adequate verification, it will also be necessary to set up a robust and well-defined system for enforcing an abolition regime, if the nuclear weapons states are to have confidence that they can safely give up their weapons. Some of the issues here are only beginning to be explored. Most of the commentators admit that it is difficult to predict at this point what it will take or what might be negotiated, but it will need to be more thoroughgoing than what we now have.[28] Moreover, the consensus view is that, unlike most treaties, withdrawal from an abolition treaty must be prohibited.[29] Finally, accompanying an abolition convention, the use or possession of nuclear weapons and materials must, of course, be made an international crime punishable as a crime against humanity.[30]

Conventional Force Reductions

Last, as a necessary adjunct to nuclear disarmament, in order to secure such an agreement, it will no doubt be necessary to reach agreement on reducing conventional arms,[31] especially offensive weapons.[32]

As to the precise size and shape of such conventional arms reductions, it is impossible to predict in advance what might be successfully negotiated.[33]

Side-Benefits

Although all the above will be a lot of work, it has been pointed out that there will be various "spin-off benefits" from such efforts: "Thus, the mechanisms and possible new bodies created by our efforts could, if successful, find additional roles in resolution of disputes, regional security problems, and other international challenges that have eluded solution."[34] Indeed, an accord on security matters would undoubtedly facilitate cooperation on all sorts of global problems.

Pathways to Abolition

As to how to get all nations to agree to go all the way down to zero. It is submitted that once we have reached minimal deterrence levels, the last stage of getting to zero may be easier than sometimes imagined. Once the Big Three—the USA, Russia, and China—agree, the rest will follow, even the hard cases of France, Israel, and Pakistan. After all, we know that Pakistan got its nuclear weapons in response to India's; India got theirs because of China's (their nuclear program began the same year as China's first nuclear test), and China got theirs because of Russia's and the USA's. So the only way that countries like Pakistan will give up their nuclear weapons is if all other countries give up theirs.

Finally, contrary to what some analysts suggest, it will not be necessary to actually resolve all the outstanding conflicts in the world in order to secure a nuclear weapons abolition convention; rather, it will only be necessary to secure an effective international dispute resolution system.[35]

As an immediate next step toward abolition, a treaty prohibiting the use of nuclear weapons would be a very good idea. The operative language of the treaty could be one sentence: "The States Parties DO HEREBY MUTUALLY FORESWEAR the use or threatened use of nuclear weapons against any State which is or becomes a Party to this treaty." Questions as to the interpretation of the treaty would be submitted to the compulsory jurisdiction of the International Court of Justice. Such a treaty would be (a) easier to adopt than a ban on possession (a mere two countries could start the process), and (b) a natural psychological bridge to complete abolition.[36]

There are, of course, numerous other short-term steps that could be taken whenever we begin to get serious about abolition.[37]

Nevertheless, with much effort and some luck, we are about to enter a whole new world, one in which we finally develop the moral clarity to view nuclear weapons as irredeemably evil, in which the $100 billion now spent annually on the world's nuclear weapons[38] can be turned to the many needs of humanity, and alternative dispute resolution systems are used to resolve international conflict.

Notes

1 Despite this encouraging statement, the fact remains that irrespective of the stated nuclear posture review statements of the superpowers, it is inevitable that if deterrence fails, each side will fight to win.
2 See www.globalzero.org. See also Philip Taubman, The Partnership: Five Cold Warriors and Their Quest to Ban the Bomb, at 12 (2012).
3 Most notably Jonathan Schell. His classic 1982 book *The Fate of the Earth* was a clarion call for abolition, which motivated many now active in the movement for abolition. See also Jonathan Schell, The Gift of Time: The Case for Abolishing Nuclear Weapons Now (1998). Cf. also Roger and Earl A. Molander, Nuclear War: What's In It For You? (1982) (another classic) and Lawrence S. Wittner, Confronting the Bomb: A Short History of the World Nuclear Disarmament Movement (2009).
4 A flood of recent books all urge abolition. See, e.g., Ray Acheson, ed., Beyond Arms Control: Challenges and Choices for Nuclear Disarmament (2010); Ken Berry, Patricia Lewis, Benoit Pelopidas, Nikolai Sokov, & Ward Wilson, Delegitimizing Nuclear Weapons: Examining the Validity of Nuclear Deterrence (2010); Barry M. Blechman & Alexander K. Bollfrass, eds., Elements of a Nuclear Disarmament Treaty: Unblocking the Road to Zero (2010); Joseph Cirincione, Nuclear Nightmares: Securing the World Before It Is Too Late (2013); Tad Daley, Apocalypse Never: Forging the Path to a Nuclear Weapon-Free World (2010); Merav Datan, Felicity Hill, Jurgen Schjeffran, & Alyn Ware, Securing Our Survival: The Case for a Nuclear Weapons Convention (2007); Gareth Evans & Yoriko Kawaguchi, eds., Eliminating Nuclear Threats: A Practical Agenda for Global Policymakers (2009); Commander Robert Green, Security without Nuclear Deterrence (2010); Corey Hinderstein, ed., Cultivating Confidence: Verification, Monitoring, and Enforcement for a World Free of Nuclear Weapons (2010); Catherine McArdle Kelleher & Judith Reppy, eds., Getting to Zero: The Path to Nuclear Disarmament (2011); David Krieger, ed., The Challenge of Abolishing Nuclear Weapons (2010); Tanya Ogilvie-White & David Santoro, Slaying the Nuclear Dragon: Disarmament Dynamics in the Twenty-First Century (2012); Michael E. O'Hanlon, A Skeptic's Case for Nuclear Disarmament (2010); George Perkovich & James M. Acton, eds., Abolishing Nuclear Weapons: A Debate (2009); William J. Perry, My Journey at the Nuclear Brink (2015); Richard Rhodes, Arsenals of Folly: The Making of the Nuclear Arms Race (2007); Richard Rhodes, The Twilight of the Bombs: Recent Challenges, New Dangers,

and the Prospects for a World without Nuclear Weapons (2010); Douglas Roche, How We Stopped Loving the Bomb: An Insider's Account of the World on the Brink of Banning Nuclear Arms (2011); Elaine Scarry, Thermonuclear Monarchy: Choosing between Democracy and Doom (2014); Eric Schlosser, Command and Control (2013); George P. Schultz, Steven P. Andreasen, Sidney D. Drell, & James E. Goodby, eds., Reykjavik Revisited: Steps Toward a World Free of Nuclear Weapons (2008); George P. Schultz & James E. Goodby, The War That Must Never Be Fought: Dilemmas of Nuclear Deterrence (2015); Nina Tannenwald, The Nuclear Taboo: The United States and the Non-Use of Nuclear Weapons Since 1945 (2007); Rob van Riet, ed., Moving Beyond Nuclear Deterrence to a Nuclear Weapons Free World (2013); and William Walker, A Perpetual Menace: Nuclear Weapons and International Order (2012). See also David A Koplow, "What Would Zero Look Like? A Treaty for the Abolition of Nuclear Weapons," 45 *Geo. J. Int'l Law* 683 (2014).

5 See www.icanw.org/polls (polls showing, variously, 77% and 87% of the American public favor abolition).

6 According to my calculations, using the deaths inflicted by a 14-kt bomb upon Hiroshima (average estimate is 120,000) as a measure, the current megatonnage of nuclear weapons of 5,000 megatons would be capable of killing 42.9-billion people. Total world population is only 7 billion.

7 Gareth Evans & Yoriko Kawaguchi, eds., supra, at 3, 27.

8 See Chapter 1 supra.

9 James E. Doyle, "Eyes on the Prize: A Strategy for Enhancing Global Security," in Perkovich & Acton, supra, at 222 (Doyle is in the Nuclear Nonproliferation Division of Los Alamos National Laboratory).

10 An inquiry to Secretary Shultz's office revealed that his source for this snappy come-backer was President Reagan himself. He said that it was "simply a repeat of what President Reagan said many times." Email communication from Susan Schendel, assistant to George Shultz (May 8, 2011).

11 Nor is this the only "doom and gloom" possibility. A recent study finds that even a small-to-medium 100-nuke "exchange" between India and Pakistan (latest estimates are that India has 80 nukes and Pakistan has 110) could result in a worldwide nuclear winter crippling agriculture for up to ten years. See Jonathan Schell, The Seventh Decade: The New Shape of Nuclear Danger, at 15 (2007). Cf. also Vipin Narang, "Posturing for Peace? Pakistan's Nuclear Postures and South Asian Stability," 34 *Int'l Security* 38 (2010) (Pakistan's nuclear posture entails decentralized command and control, which creates a "nontrivial" risk of inadvertent use of nuclear weapons, especially given India's "Cold Start" doctrine).

12 Even the most hard-headed of Cold War warriors, such as Paul Nitze. In 1999, at age 92, in his last op-ed, Nitze announced his change of mind in favor of abolition. See J. Peter Scoblic, "Disarmament Redux," *Bulletin of the Atomic Scientists* (Mar/April 2008), at 35.

13 Herbert York, supra, Chapter 1 at note 21.

14 Securing Our Survival, supra, at 17. Cf. Elaine Scarry, Thermonuclear Monarchy: Choosing between Democracy and Doom, at 397 (2014) (Gen. Kevin P. Chilton: "This [nuclear mission] is a mission area where we as human beings are challenged to be perfect. We are not perfect.").

15 While that is still true of books, there have been several recent confer- ences on the "humanitarian consequences" of nuclear weapons as well as conferences on their immorality and illegality. See Beatrice Fihn, "A New Humanitarian Era: Prohibiting the Unacceptable," *Arms Control Today* (July/August 2015). See also Nina Tannenwald, The Nuclear Taboo: The United States and the Non-Use of Nuclear Weapons Since 1945 (2007) (taboo "associated with a sense of moral opprobrium regarding such weapons").

16 E. Scarry, supra, at 404.

17 Philip Allott, "The Emerging Universal Legal System," 3 *Int'l L. Forum* 12, 12 (2001).

18 See, e.g., Laurie Grossman, "U.S., Soviet Teens Rank Nuclear War as a Major Fear," *Wash. Post* August 18, 1988 (studies point to an "alarming degree of futurelessness," according to lead author Dr. Eric Chivian) and Kari Poikolainen, Terhi Aalto-Setala, Annamari Tuulia-Henriksson, Mauri Marttunen, & Jouko Lonnqvist, "Fear of nuclear war increases the risk of common mental disorders among young adults: a five-year follow-up study," www.biomedicalcentral.com/1471-2458/4/42. Cf. also Andrea Dudikova, "Fiery suicides baffle Czechs," *Philadelphia Inquirer* November 16, 2003, p. A17 (one suicide note referenced "world filled with violence").

19 See Harald Muller, "Enforcement of the Rules in a Nuclear Weapon-Free World," Chapter 2 in Corey Hinderstein, supra, at 34, 39–40, 54–55, & 58–60 (At 55: "relying on...virtual arsenals carries the risk of preventing one of the most important preconditions for a zero-nuclear world from emerging, namely a robust framework of trust") and Jonathan Schell, The Gift of Time, supra, at 140–147 (excellent discussion). But see O'Hanlon, supra, at 5, 9–10, 18–20, 24, 82–84, 95–107 (while "[c]apricious or blatantly self-serving reconstitution must be avoided," the ability to rebuild is "an asset...not a liability.").

20 This argument has been set forth most fully by Keith Payne. See Brookings Institution, "The Nuclear Posture Review and the Future of Nuclear Weapons," at 13–15 (March 29, 2010, conference transcript) and Keith B. Payne, "The Case against Nuclear Abolition and for Nuclear Deterrence," *Comparative Strategy* 17 (January 1998), at 3–43.

21 Barry M. Blechman, "Why We Need to Eliminate Nuclear Weapons— And How to Do It," Chapter 1 in Elements of a Nuclear Disarmament Treaty, supra, at 8–9. Accord, John Mueller, Atomic Obsession: Nuclear Alarmism from Hiroshima to Al-Queda, Chapter 3 (2010).

22 See, e.g., Daley, supra, Chapter 8.

23 The best collection of such arguments is found in Schell's Gift of Time, supra, at 31–34.

24 Daley, at 190. Cf. also Alexander K. Bollfrass, "Breaking Out of Zero: Would Cheating Be Worth the Risk?," Chapter 8 in Blechman & Bollfrass, supra; and Muller, supra, at 39, 53.

25 Daley, at 191. Cf. id. At 200–201 (Gen. Lee Butler notes that such an inter- national outlaw would risk being removed, forcibly if necessary).

26 Id. At 191–194 (proving the point with historical instances).

27 See, e.g., Corey Hinderstein, supra; Steve Fetter & Ivan Oelrich, "Verifying a Prohibition on Nuclear Weapons," Chapter 2 in Blechman & Bollfrass,

supra; Perkovich & Acton, supra, Chapter 2; and www.state.gov/t/avc/ ipndv (new "International Partnership for Nuclear Verification" between Department of State and Nuclear Threat Initiative). Also, top experts are agreed that "as an adjunct to any nuclear disarmament treaty, it would be essential to create international institutions to operate and safeguard both enrichment and processing plants (if they cannot be eliminated altogether) and spent fuel storage sites." International Panel on Fissile Materials, Global Fissile Material Report 2009: A Path to Nuclear Disarmament, at 113 (2009).

28 Cf. generally, Muller, supra, Chapter 2 (may need some institution other than the veto-impaired UN Security Council, or have a treaty provision disallowing use of veto re the abolition treaty); James E. Goodby, "Internationalizing the Nuclear Fuel Cycle," Chapter 10 in Shultz et al., Reykjavik Revisited, at 363–366 (various ideas, including Jessica Mathews proposal for robust "Inspections Implementation Force"); and Securing Our Survival, supra, at 90, 175 (compliance and dispute settlement procedures of model convention; need for changes in "international governance" merely noted without specifics).

29 See, e.g., Muller, at 49.

30 See, e.g., Rebecca Bornstein, "Enforcing a Nuclear Disarmament Treaty," Chapter 6 in Blechman & Bollfrass, Elements, supra, at 159. And enforced via a UN Peace Force. See Raymond J. Juzaitis & John E. McLaughlin, "Challenges of Verification and Compliance within a State of Universal Latency," Chapter 4 in Shultz et al., Reykjavik Revisited, supra, at 199 and Chapter 10 infra.

31 The Russians will otherwise object to nuclear disarmament. See Mikhail Gorbachev, The New Russia, at 304 (2016) ("If we do not address the issue of ... reductions of [conventional] arms ... all talk of a nuclear-free world will come to nothing.").

32 Arms control experts have long distinguished offensive arms from those strictly defensive in nature, such as fixed anti-tank emplacements. See, e.g., Jonathan Schell, The Abolition, at 176–177 (1984); Harold Feivesen, Richard Ullman, & Frank von Hippel, "Reducing U.S. and Soviet Arsenals," 41 *Bulletin of Atomic Scientists* 144 (August 1985); Robert Johansen, Toward an Alternative Security System, at 22–24 (1983); and Mark Sommer, Beyond the Bomb: Living without Nuclear Weapons, at 52–55 (1985). As pointed out by Schell, even "missile defense" could add to stability under a zero-nuke regime. In the short run, however, missile defense (assuming it even works) is destabilizing, creating fears of a first-strike capability, and therefore counterproductive to arms reductions. See William Walker, A Perpetual Menace: Nuclear Weapons and International Order, at 100 (2012).

33 Agreement on this issue may depend on securing agreement on a UN peace force. See Chapter 10 infra.
  A new and "unconventional" conventional force—cyber war—also needs to be prohibited by treaty. See Richard A. Clarke & Robert K. Knake, Cyber War: The Next Threat to National Security and What to do about It, at 266–269 (2010); Danny Vinik, "America's secret arsenal," *Politico* (December 9, 2015) (US has "most powerful cyberattack capabilities in the world; Rep. Jim Himes and others propose treaty); Bruce G. Blair, "Why

Our Nuclear Weapons Can Be Hacked," *New York Times* (March 14, 2017) (need to "put nuclear networks off limits to cyberintrusion"); and "Why everything is hackable," *The Economist*, April 8, 2017, at 69 ("Department of Defense has found significant vulnerabilities in every weapon system it has examined.").

34 Edward Ifft, "Political Dimensions of Determining 'Effective' Verification," Chapter 1 in Hinderstein, supra, at 29.

35 See Chapter 9 infra. Among the few glancing references to this idea in the literature, see, e.g., Evans & Kawaguchi, supra, at 198 ("The development of more cooperative approaches to conflict prevention and resolution may well prove more productive...than focusing entirely on arms limitation measures.").

36 See Alyn Ware, "From nuclear taboo to a prohibition (ban) on use: The next step to nuclear-weapon-free world?" (Basel Peace Office, 2015); Middle Powers Initiative, "Framework Forum: Issues and proposals for taking forward nuclear disarmament" (Geneva, April 18, 2016) (Daryl Kimball, President of Arms Control Association, favors use ban to "strengthen the legal norm against the use of nuclear weapons and put pressure on the nuclear weapon States to reduce the role of nuclear weapons in their security doctrines"); Kingston Reif, "Momentum builds for nuclear ban treaty," *Arms Control Today*, vol. 46 no. 5, pp. 26, 27 (June 2016) (Annika Thunborg, Disarmament Director, Sweden, says use ban could gain acceptance from nuclear weapons states); and UNGA Resol. 50/71 (Draft Convention on the Prohibition of the Use of Nuclear Weapons, December 12, 1995). A step in this same direction would be a no-first-use treaty. See George P. Shultz & James E. Goodby, The War That Must Never Be Fought: Dilemmas of Nuclear Deterrence, at 356, 368 (2015). Cf. Hans Bethe, "Containing Deterrence: Arms Control after Reykjavik," 4 *New Perspectives Quarterly* 26, 29 (Spring 1987) (Bethe joins McNamara, McGeorge Bundy, Kennan, and Gerard Smith in favoring "no first use").

37 See Chapter 12 infra at nn. 37-41 (including CTBT, FMCT, and the new ban treaty).

38 Religions for Peace, "A Nuclear-Weapon-Free World: Our Common Good" (August 6, 2015), www.religionsforpeace.org.

9 International dispute resolution mechanisms

What will it take to replace the war system with the global rule of law? There are two critical components to "world peace through law": (1) a comprehensive and effective international dispute resolution system, and (2) effective enforcement mechanisms. This chapter looks at the former, the next chapter at the latter.

Two of the most prominent world federalists in America, Grenville Clark[1] and Professor Louis B. Sohn,[2] co-authored the classic work on world federalism, "World Peace Through World Law: Two Alternative Plans."[3] They set forth the argument for "pacific settlement of disputes" as follows:

> The nations of the world can be expected to renounce force or the threat of force as a means of dealing with international disputes only if adequate alternative means are provided for the peaceful settlement of these controversies. This is the age-old experience as to disputes between individuals and communities within a nation. It is no less true of international disputes.
>
> …
>
> Accordingly, the United Nations must not be limited to the suppression of attempts to change existing conditions by force after the violence has occurred or is imminent. On the contrary, it should be clearly understood that all violent efforts to change the existing order can be prevented in the long run only by providing adequate and flexible means for peaceful change such as negotiation, mediation, arbitration, conciliation and adjudication, or such a combination of these as may be most suitable to the particular case. To this end it is plain that carefully organized world institutions are essential.[4]

Clark and Sohn note that it is not sufficient for the maintenance of peace that there be total disarmament "even when supplemented by an effective world police." It is also "essential to equip the United Nations with more comprehensive and improved machinery to deal at an early stage with all important international controversies."[5] Hence, they propose not only an International Court of Justice but also a World Conciliation Board and a World Equity Tribunal.[6]

These dispute settlement mechanisms are part of Clark and Sohn's larger proposal for a world federalist superstructure. But Professor Sohn was not an all-or-nothing world federalist; rather, he was willing to consider passage of a part of their larger proposal. Thus, he accepted a commission from an ABA Standing Committee on World Order Under Law to create a Draft General Treaty on the Peaceful Settlement of International Disputes. The draft Proposal, approved by the ABA House of Delegates in 1984, is mainly a collection of mere precatory statements urging, without compulsion, States Parties to resort to an array of alternative dispute-resolution mechanisms, including negotiation, good offices, mediation, commissions of inquiry, arbitration, regional agencies, or judicial settlement.[7] Similarly, the UN Charter, while seemingly mandating resort to a variety of alternative dispute resolution mechanisms,[8] ends up making resort to any of these procedures merely at the discretion of the Security Council and the parties themselves.[9]

Neither the ABA proposal nor the current UN Charter provisions go far enough. What is necessary is a comprehensive system of compulsory international dispute resolution, proceeding in four stepwise stages with (1) compulsory negotiation, (2) compulsory mediation, (3) compulsory arbitration, and (4) compulsory adjudication.[10] As to what would make resort to international dispute resolution "compulsory," the answer would have to be not only a treaty but also a powerful international norm making it so,[11] an international norm considerably more powerful than that associated with the 1929 Kellogg-Briand Treaty.[12] A WPTL treaty would, of course, need to define with considerable precision what triggers the duty to engage in international dispute resolution as well as mechanisms to deal with the party who refuses to enter into international dispute resolution where it is mandated.[13]

Compulsory negotiation. Almost no attention has been paid by international legal scholars to the role that compulsory negotiation could play in the resolution of international conflict.[14] But historians who have studied the matter carefully have concluded that mere negotiation alone might very well have prevented WWI.[15] Furthermore, negotiation alone (in the form of the much-maligned "UN talk shop") has almost certainly prevented several major wars.[16] Thus, the important role that mere compulsory negotiation alone could play in preventing war ought not to be underestimated. But if compulsory negotiation did not resolve the conflict, the state parties would then move on to the second stage of international dispute resolution: compulsory international mediation.

Compulsory mediation. Compulsory mediation has a tremendous potential for avoiding wars of all kinds, both inter-state and civil wars. According to former UN Secretary General Kofi Annan, "[o]ver the last two decades more wars have ended through mediation than in the previous two centuries."[17] As useful as voluntary international mediation has proven, what is needed to secure lasting peace is a strong norm (and treaty) mandating compulsory mediation and the ready availability of institutions to which resort can be had.

Mediation is simple, merely requiring the two sides to agree upon a mediator, who has no powers to compel either side to do anything, relying instead upon the voluntary agreement of both sides.[18] Mediation is capable of assuming many forms, e.g., "advisory arbitration," which might lend itself well to resolving international conflict. Although some volunteer groups provide free international mediation,[19] this is something which obviously should be largely funded by the international community.

In the United States, the use of mediation in domestic courts has increased tenfold in the past two decades,[20] with mediation being mandatory in some states before a plaintiff is afforded access to a jury trial, with the result that in such jurisdictions 85% of all cases are settled during mediation.[21] It is high time to transfer this successful record to the international level.[22] In sum, if the countries of the world signed a treaty requiring only one thing—compulsory mediation—we would have an infinitely safer world.

Compulsory arbitration. Conflicts not resolved by compulsory mediation would move on to the third stage of international dispute resolution: compulsory arbitration. Like negotiation and mediation, arbitration has been somewhat neglected by many international legal scholars, who have chosen to focus most of their attention on an international court.[23] But arbitration has a much longer and more productive history, dating back several millennia.[24] According to Thucydides, "it was impossible to attack as an enemy someone who was ready to respond before an arbitral tribunal."[25] Thousands of international arbitrations were held in the Middle Ages,[26] and since the famous Jay Treaty of 1794, hundreds of successful arbitrations have been held,[27] most notably the *Alabama Claims* arbitration of 1871–1872, as a result of which the United Kingdom paid the United States the sum of $15.5 million in damages for permitting the construction of warships for the Confederacy.[28] Although tremendous efforts were expended to attempt to secure the idea of compulsory international arbitration during the Hague conferences of 1899 and 1907, ultimately it was rejected.[29] Moreover, since that time, proposals for compulsory international arbitration have failed several times, being peremptorily rejected by President Woodrow Wilson at the 1919 Paris Peace Conference,[30] vetoed by the United States in 1924,[31] and subsequently deleted from a preliminary draft of the UN Charter.[32]

Part of the problem, it would seem, is that because of the exaggerated claims made by some in the peace movement as to what the Hague Conventions actually accomplished,[33] the unfortunate result was that when WWI was not prevented by anything in the Hague Conventions, "arbitration" was unfairly blamed when in fact it had never been tried.[34]

Arbitration provides much greater flexibility than adjudication, offering the parties various options in the selection of arbitrators, including having specialized experts on the panel; of holding the hearings in secret or keeping the results secret; of tailoring the issues to be considered; and generally controlling the details of the procedure to be used in ways not dependent upon territorial jurisdiction.[35] For those not satisfied with the results of arbitration, international adjudication would serve as a backup to international arbitration, resort to it serving as a kind of appellate remedy.[36]

Compulsory adjudication. The final stage of international dispute resolution is compulsory adjudication. Despite initial high hopes that the International Court of Justice would "have a central place in the plans of the United Nations for the settlement of international disputes by peaceful means,"[37] it has not worked out that way. Rather, the ICJ as currently constituted has turned out to be a distinct disappointment.[38] Only 67 countries currently accept the ICJ's compulsory jurisdiction, and the ICJ lacks independent enforcement powers.[39] Thus, states have sometimes refused to submit to its jurisdiction or comply with its judgments.[40] Most significantly from the standpoint of our essential goal of securing world peace, of the Permanent Five on the Security Council, all but the United Kingdom have now withdrawn from the ICJ's compulsory jurisdiction.[41] Moreover, a certain number of the ICJ's decisions have been less than satisfactory, causing a critical loss of confidence in the Court.[42] In sum, many commentators have almost given up on the Court, at least as an effective organ for peace, merely making suggestions for improvements at the margins.[43]

In view, then, of the history of the ICJ, it would seem that to push the idea of creating an even more ambitious Court—with compulsory jurisdiction and broad equity powers—is to demand the impossible.

Troubling questions

Indeed, some distinguished international law scholars argue that an improved ICJ would be impossible. Perhaps the most cogent exposition comes from the pen of a respected former UN official, Professor Oscar Schachter:

> It is no great mystery why they [nations] are reluctant to have their disputes adjudicated. Litigation is uncertain, time consuming, troublesome. Political officials do not want to lose control of a case that they might resolve by negotiation or political pressures. Diplomats naturally prefer diplomacy; political leaders value persuasion, manoeuvre and flexibility. They often prefer to "play it by ear," making their rules fit the circumstances rather than submit to pre-existing rules. Political forums, such as the United Nations, are often more attractive, especially to those likely to get wide support for political reasons. We need only compare the large number of disputes brought to the United Nations with the few submitted to adjudication ... States do not want to risk losing a case when the stakes are high or be troubled with litigation in minor matters. An international tribunal may not inspire confidence, especially when some judges are seen as "political" or as hostile. There is apprehension that the law is too malleable or fragmented to sustain "true" judicial decisions. In some situations, the legal issues are viewed as but one element in a complex political situation and consequently it is considered unwise or futile to deal with them separately. Finally, we note the underlying perception of many governments that law essentially supports the *status quo* and that courts are not responsive to demands for justice or change.[44]

And again, the same author:

> Only a raving optimist could expect a transformation in the foreseeable future to the system of enforceable law envisioned in the rhetoric of Nuremberg ... Neither governments nor their peoples are ready, by and large, to entrust their security and vital interest to foreign judges or international organs.[45]

Another very reputable international legal scholar, Professor Julius Stone, Australian Professor of Jurisprudence and International Law, raises some serious concerns about the Clark-Sohn proposals for a World Conciliation Board and a World Equity Tribunal:

> Even careful proposals of this sort overreach present possibilities in at least three major respects. First, they assume that States can be induced, in one step, to move from attempted control, each of their own destiny, to surrender to an impartial third party of the power to determine the basic conditions on which their destiny may depend. Second, they assume that there are available the personnel necessary to provide the wise arbiters of which such a Tribunal, in order to have even a chance of success, must consist. Third, they assume that the ideas of "justice" or "equity" in their present form and content will provide a standard usable by the Tribunal and acceptable to the Parties.[46]

Professor Stone notes further that most past international arbitrations were (a) on relatively narrow points as to which the parties knew the range of likely dispositions and found the risk of losing to be acceptable, and (b) entered into by nations whose ethical and legal systems were not too far apart. To ask countries to submit all future disputes of unknown nature and as to unknown parties is simply asking too much.[47] Stone, who is a self-described "skeptic" about the "highly formal-conceptualist" idealistic proposals for submitting all inter-state disputes to third-party judgment, believes that "[t]o press recklessly beyond [the] feasible tasks" of functionalist problem-solving in areas such as conservation and development risks disaster.[48] In sum, Julius Stone believed that "[t]he refusal by States to accept third-party judgment in the wide range of conflicts which most threaten international peace is a stark fact of life…[a]nd no hopes for the rule of law…are likely to make it disappear."[49]

The above arguments against WPTL are carefully reasoned and persuasively made by thoughtful mainstream international law scholars. Even "liberal" international law scholars have been skeptical of establishing the global rule of law. Most famously, Professor Richard Falk has posited the "tragic paradox" of international law as follows: "The necessity for effective management of violence in world affairs exists alongside the impossibility of achieving management by consensual means."[50]

Some answers

It may well be impossible to secure a comprehensive international dispute resolution system unless it is accompanied or preceded by a treaty for nuclear disarmament. Not only would such an agreement give nation-states the necessary confidence to rely upon international dispute resolution, but such a historic accord might also provide the moral impetus needed.[51] Further, an abolition treaty would inevitably already have dispute resolution mechanisms attached to it.[52] Thus, all it would take to have a solid security architecture is to expand such provisions into a comprehensive system for international dispute resolution. Even shy of that, however, the UN Security Council now has the power under Chapter VII of the Charter to order parties to a dispute threatening the peace to enter alternative dispute resolution.[53]

Moreover, there is another very important reason why progress need not await such a comprehensive agreement: Professor Sohn points out that countries can opt into any portions of the alternative dispute resolution system at their own pace, e.g., initially agreeing to only compulsory mediation.[54]

Furthermore, thinking strategically, we can focus our attention on certain key countries, specifically, Russia and the United States, which together hold over 90% of the nuclear weapons on the planet. If these two countries alone agreed to the compulsory jurisdiction of the ICJ, would that not be incredibly significant? Of course, it would. Well, it just so happens that former Soviet President Mikhail Gorbachev already proposed compulsory jurisdiction for the ICJ in 1987.[55] So not only is the idea of establishing a comprehensive regime of global dispute resolution not unrealistic, the single most important and difficult part of it might be easy to accomplish.[56]

Equity jurisdiction

We have argued, with Clark and Sohn, that we need a World Court with compulsory jurisdiction and power to hear both "law" and "equity" claims, whether such claims are viewed as "justiciable" or not.[57] While it is true that such broad equity jurisdiction would be worrying as to certain existential issues[58] and would raise the usual concerns about the legitimacy of judges "legislating,"[59] if we are serious about resolving all international conflict, nothing less than full equity jurisdiction even as to so-called "non-justiciable" issues will suffice.[60] It is time for international law to move to a more mature and confident stage of development, just as domestic courts gradually adopted equity jurisdiction.[61]

Working out the details

The ultimate goal—world peace through law—is clear, and when one looks closely at what would be involved, quite feasible and practical.

Of course, the above discussion is merely a broad outline of what would be required. A comprehensive working out of the above general concepts will require the work of many others with a wide variety of expertise. For example, the precise relationship between arbitration and adjudication would need to be worked out with care. Perhaps, given the serious national security concerns that could be involved, the default position (absent both parties agreeing to the contrary) ought to be that international arbitration should be purely advisory.[62]

Various structural issues would also need to be addressed.[63] Commentators are already suggesting the possibility of regional courts,[64] of an international version of a small claims court,[65] as well as creative use of "chambers" practice (the ICJ statute allows special chambers of the Court to be established), perhaps to handle cases involving varying mixtures of "law" and "equity" or requiring special expertise.[66]

One suggestion, administratively, is to establish an Office of Dispute Resolution housed in or near the UN or, more likely, in regional offices, staffed with knowledgeable and user-friendly people, who could outline all alternative dispute resolution mechanisms available and, with the parties' permission, make tentative suggestions as to how they may wish to proceed. These offices could be available upon request or, in special emergency circumstances, sua sponte or upon Security Council direction (this would allow, e.g., one or more parties to save face by not having to themselves initiate even these preliminary proceedings). Such a screening and advisory intake operation could be immensely helpful to the parties. It could get things off on the right foot, helping assure that things are headed in an appropriate direction (e.g., realizing that other parties may need to be involved, or that immediate referral to the Security Council may be advisable). Tremendous expertise has been accumulated over the years by private and public professionals in a wide variety of alternative dispute resolution techniques, including various combinations thereof,[67] and this administrative body (or bodies) could make full use of this knowledge in helping the parties to an expeditious and efficient start toward resolving their dispute.

An Office of Dispute Resolution could also be charged with at least initiating the enforcement of compliance with the mandate of international dispute resolution, with sanctions, or recommended sanctions, up to and including something in the nature of a default judgment in case of a party's refusal to enter into international dispute resolution in good faith.[68]

International mediation and arbitration should be readily available at low cost. Just as domestic courts are available to parties upon payment of minimal fees in the interest of providing justice, similarly international alternative dispute resolution mechanisms should be made readily available in the interest of providing international justice. As these public dispute resolution capacities become more sophisticated and are regularly used, they will reinforce the habit of making use of them and increase the likelihood of their usage as much as any treaty could.[69]

In addition to these regional conflict resolution centers, there should be regional conflict prevention centers, possibly located at universities, which could apply the latest conflict prevention techniques.[70] Using these and other techniques for conflict avoidance,[71] we would move closer to a world of lasting peace.

Where we are headed

Where we are heading is clear: a world subject to the global rule of law. Starting with existing international legal structures, such as the International Criminal Court,[72] the Law of the Sea Tribunal, the WTO's Appellate Body, and eventually even an International Human Rights Court,[73] the proposed international dispute resolution system would provide a comprehensive system of world peace through law. As stated by former United Nations Under-Secretary-General, Brian Urquhart:

> A rule-based international society may seem a lackluster phrase, but it describes, for those who wish organized life on this planet to survive in a decent form, the most important of all the long-term international objectives mankind can have.[74]

Notes

1 Harvard Law, 1906; consultant to Secretary of War Stimson, 1940–1944.
2 Bemis Professor of International Law, Harvard. Cf. John E. Noyes, "In Memoriam: Louis B. Sohn," 2011–2012 American Branch Proceedings 211 (2013) ("Louis B. Sohn was a giant in the field of international law...").
3 1st ed. 1958; 3rd ed. 1966.
4 Clark & Sohn, at 89 (3rd ed. 1966) (emphases in the original).
5 Id. at 89–90.
6 Id. at 91.
   Clark and Sohn were not the first to come up with the idea for an equity tribunal. In 1907, a Central American Court of Justice was created by treaty between Costa Rica, Guatemala, Honduras, Nicaragua, and Salvador, providing for compulsory arbitration of "all controversies...of whatsoever nature." The treaty lasted for ten years and worked "surprisingly well." Shirley V. Scott, International Law, US Power: The United States' Quest for Legal Security, at 60–61 (2012).

 7 Typical of such language is Article 5(3), which provides that if the Security
   Council has recommended a particular procedure and that has not resolved the dispute, then any party can return to the Security Council and
   ask for another recommended procedure and the parties "shall make a
   special effort to settle the dispute by that procedure."
 8 Article 33(1) provides: "The parties to any dispute, the continuance of
   which is likely to endanger the maintenance of international peace and security, shall, first of all, seek a solution by negotiation, enquiry, mediation,
   conciliation, arbitration, judicial settlement, resort to regional agencies
   or arrangements, or other peaceful means of their own choice" (emphasis
   added).
 9 Article 33(2) provides: "The Security Council shall, when it deems necessary, call upon the parties to settle their dispute by such means" (emphasis
   added).
10 Parties could skip stages upon mutual agreement. Also, negotiation would
   obviously be an option at any stage of the proceedings.
11 See Michael Signer, Demagogue: The Fight to Save Democracy from Its
   Worst Enemies, at 103–106 (2009) (underlying mores are more important
   than laws [citing de Tocqueville]).
12 See Robert H. Ferrell, Peace in Their Time: The Origins of the Kellogg-
   Briand Pact (1952) (vast majority of contemporary statesmen viewed it as a
   cynical ploy to placate strong anti-war sentiment after WWI; earlier draft
   of treaty which would have provided mediation and arbitration rejected
   by the United Kingdom) and Adam Tooze, The Deluge: The Great War,
   America and the Remaking of the Global Order, 1916–1931, at 473–475
   (2014) (British and French view Pact as "an American evasion" due to
   lack of enforcement provisions). But see David A. Koplow, "A Nuclear
   Kellogg-Briand Pact: Proposing a Treaty for the Renunciation of Nuclear
   War as an Instrument of National Policy," 42 *Syracuse J. of Int'l Law &
   Commerce* 123 (2014) (argues that Kellogg-Briand "has gotten a bum rap"
   and deserves a new lease on life).
13 See text at note 68 infra (possible default judgment or similar procedures)
   and Chapter 10 infra at nn. 66, 67 (problem of "outliers).
14 But cf. Simon O'Connor & Cecilia Baillet, "The Good Faith Obligation to
   Maintain International Peace and Security and the Pacific Settlement of
   Disputes," Chapter 4, at 70–71, in Cecilia Marcela Baillet & Kjetil Majezinovic
   Larsen, eds., Promoting Peace through International Law (2015).
15 See, e.g., Louis Lusky, "Four Problems in Lawmaking for Peace," 80 *Pol.
   Sc. Q. 341*, 341 (1965). See also Adam Hochschild, To End All Wars: A
   Story of Loyalty and Rebellion 1914–1918, at 275 (2011) ("If there were ever
   a war that should have had an early negotiated peace, it was this one …
   Could there ever have been a more improbable chain of events than the
   one from the assassination at Sarajevo to an entire continent in flames a
   mere six weeks later? And why, in that case, could it not be undone?").
16 See Lusky, supra. Cf. Jonas Gahr Store, "Why We Must Talk," *New York
   Review of Books*, April 7, 2011, at 51–54.
17 Isak Svensson & Peter Wallensteen, The Go-between: Jan Eliasson and the
   Styles of Mediation, at ix (2010). For the prior history, see Kalevi J. Holsti,
   Peace and War: Armed Conflicts and International Order 1638–1989, at 111,
   136, 162 (1991) (many wars mediated in 1700s, but not yet used to prevent

wars; no mention of mediation in treaties of 1814–1815; Treaty of Paris [1856] made the first reference to the pacific settlement of disputes since the Treaty of Westphalia and Protocol 23 thereof included "a general statement to the effect that governments should resort to mediation…before they could legitimately use force"). As to the ineffectiveness of not mediating, see, e.g., Stephen Kinzer, All the Shah's Men: An American Coup and the Roots of Middle East Terror (2003) (Eisenhower misled by incomplete information into agreeing to CIA coup of Prime Minister Mohammed Mossadegh, rejecting an offer of mediation, with tragic consequences [arguably including 9/11] down to the present day) and William J. Perry, "How to Make a Deal with North Korea," *Politico Magazine*, April 15, 2017 ("we were tantalizingly close to an agreement" at the end of the Clinton administration when George W. Bush abandoned diplomacy for a more confrontational approach, which failed).

18 Cf. generally, Merrills, Chapters 2–4 (treating separately "conciliation," a form of ADR utilizing a fact-finding commission, a procedural mechanism available for use at all four stages of international ADR) and Oliver Ramsbotham, Tom Woodhouse, and Hugh Miall, Contemporary Conflict Resolution (2nd ed. 2005) (defending conflict resolution against claims that some conflicts are not amenable, nor should they be, to conflict resolution).

19 See www.mediatorsbeyondborders.org; www.pilpg.org; and "Privatizing peace," *Economist*, July 2, 2011, p. 50 (listing other groups).

20 Cf. Christopher Mitchell & Michael Banks, Handbook of Conflict Resolution: The Analytical Problem-Solving Approach (1996) (explosive growth of ADR in the 1980s and 1990s). Similarly, the teaching of ADR in law school has increased more than tenfold. When I went to law school in the late 1960s, there were no courses; today every law school has at least one course. As to the growth of ADR in other countries, see www.hiil.org (international conferences for past 15 years).

21 Cf. William L. Ury, Jeanne M. Brett, & Stephen B. Goldberg, Getting Disputes Resolved: Designing Systems to Cut the Costs of Conflict, at 140 (1993) ("some U.S. state mediation agencies reported settlement rates of between 75 and 88 percent"). Plus, many cases not settled during the mediation itself are subsequently settled due in part to the mediation.

22 See Melanie E. Greenberg, John H. Barton, & Margaret E. McGuiness, eds., Words Over War: Mediation and Arbitration to Prevent Deadly Conflict, at 1–2 (2002) ("To our surprise we found that international courts and arbitration bodies play an important role in resolving many narrow international disputes, but they do not figure prominently in deadly conflict threatening the very nature of the states") (emphases added). Given the total neglect of WPTL concepts in the past half century, this should have been no surprise whatever.

23 See James D. Fry, "Arbitrating Arms Control Disputes," 45 *Stan. J. Int'l Law* 359 (2008) (noting relative neglect of arbitration and arguing for its greater use; also argues that arbitration is preferable to resort to Security Council on the grounds of procedural fairness and greater acceptability by recalcitrant states such as North Korea).

24 For the earliest history, cf. Amnon Altman, Tracing the Earliest Recorded Concepts of International Law: The Ancient Near East (2500-330 BCE), at 78–80 (2012) (the occasional practice of arbitration in the reign of

Hammurabi [ca. 1700 BC]). For the history of American arbitration movement, see Chapter 4 at note 1 supra.

25 Quoted in M. Lachs, "Arbitration and International Adjudication," in A.H.A. Soons, ed., International Arbitration: Past and Prospects, at 38 (1990). According to my edition of Thucydides, I find: "[W]hen one party offers [arbitration] it is quite illegal to attack him first." Thucydides, History of the Peloponnesian War, at 85 (Rex Warner transl., 1954). Of course, first the Spartans and then the Athenians ended up disobeying this supposed injunction, resulting in the aforementioned war (421-404 BC), ending the Golden Age of Greece.

26 Mark W. Janis, America and the Law of Nations 1776–1939, at 132 (2010). See id. (in 1910, Secretary of State John W. Foster opined that all three of America's Nineteenth century wars [1812, 1846, and 1848] could have been avoided if resort had been made to arbitration).

27 See M.C.W. Pinto, "The Prospects for International Arbitration: Inter-State Disputes," in A.H.A. Soons, ed., International Arbitration, supra, at 69–70.

28 President Ulysses S. Grant was delighted with this arbitration, predicting "an epoch when a court recognized in all nations will settle international differences instead of keeping large standing armies." Mark W. Janis, An Introduction to International Law, at 116 (3rd ed. 1999). See Fry, supra, at 360 (Benjamin Franklin also a proponent of international arbitration).

29 See Margaret MacMillan, The War That Ended Peace: The Road to 1914, at 300–305 (2013) (Germany went into Hague conferences determined to derail compulsory arbitration); Roger Chickering, Imperial Germany and a World without War: The Peace Movement and German Society, 1892–1914, at 227, 238–239 (1975) (Kaiser William's attitude toward arbitration: "I shall continue to rely on...my sharp sword. And shit on all their [Hague conference] decisions!"); and David D. Caron, "War and International Adjudication: Reflections on the 1899 Peace Conference," 94 *AJIL* 4, 15–18, 28 (2000).

30 See Holsti, supra, at 192–194, 202–205 (proposal by French delegate, Leon Bourgeois, for international arbitration and international army summarily rejected by Wilson in favor of his own ideas); Margaret MacMillan, Paris 1919, at 87–88 (2001) (Wilson dismissively rejects similar British proposal); Adam Tooze, The Deluge: The Great War, America and the Remaking of the Global Order, 1916–1931, at 265–267 (2014) (arbitration provisions of League not really serious because, at urging of United Kingdom and Wilson, unanimity required); and Kuehl, at 277–278, 340–342 (Taft and others unhappy that Wilson's League proposal neglected century-long effort for compulsory arbitration). Compare Warren F. Kuehl, Seeking World Order: the United States and International Organizations to 1920, at 224–226, 255–267 (1969) (Wilson ill-informed about proposals for arbitration, his senior aide Colonel House being "startled...at Wilson's lack of knowledge on the subject") with Charles Seymour, Letters From the Paris Peace Conference, at 25 (Harold B. Whiteman, Jr., 1965) (notes of meeting with Wilson: "Opposed to machinery of League to Enforce Peace. Such machinery under discussion would break down conference in a day") and Mark Mazower, Governing the World: The History of an Idea, at 121–128, 131, 134–138 (2012) (other possible reasons for Wilson's views).

31 See Tooze, supra, at 472–473 (proposal by Ramsay MacDonald and Edouard Herriot for compulsory arbitration rejected by US Secretary of State Charles Evans Hughes).

32 Holsti at 264–270 (an original proposal "in the tradition of Leon Bourgeois's ideas" for an international peace force and compulsory jurisdiction in the International Court of Justice discarded).

33 See David S. Patterson, Toward a Warless World: The Travail of the American Peace Movement 1877–1914, at 108–109, 118–121, and 160–161 (1976) (despite fact that Hague conventions did not provide for compulsory arbitration, some in peace movement hailed conventions as new Magna Carta for the world).

34 Id. at 231 and 256.

35 See J.G. Merrills, International Dispute Settlement, Chapter 5 (5th ed. 2011); Rafael Domingo, The New Global Law, at 110–112 (2010); and Jonathan I. Charney, "Third Party Dispute Settlement and International Law," 36 *Colum. Transnat. L.J.* 65, 70 (1998).

36 Extensive debates in the literature as to which is better, arbitration or adjudication, are pointless. What is needed is an integrated systemic approach that utilizes the strengths of both. Similarly irrelevant are concerns in the domestic arena as to the denial of the right to jury trial.

37 Leo Gross, "The International Court of Justice: Consideration of Requirements for Enhancing Its Role in the International Legal Order," 65 *Am. J. Int'l L.* 253, 253 n. 1 (1971) (quoting the Rapporteur of the committee presenting the ICJ statute to the UN Conference on International Organization).

38 See, e.g., Gross, supra; and John F. Murphy, The Evolving Dimensions of International Law: Hard Choices for the World Community, at 65–75 (2010) (ICJ characterized as "dysfunctional" and "broken").

39 A party can go to the Security Council to seek "measures," but the only time this was tried (by Nicaragua, in 1986), the United States vetoed the attempt. See Mary Ellen O'Connell, The Power and Purpose of International Law: Insights From the Theory and Practice of Enforcement, at 303 (2008).

40 Mark Weston Janis, "Somber Reflections on the Compulsory Jurisdiction of the International Court," 81 *Am. J. Int'l L.* 144 (1987); Leo Gross, "Underutilization of the International Court of Justice," 27 *Harv. Int'l L.J.* 571, 578–579 (1986); and Posner, supra, at 135.

41 See Posner, supra, at 140. There are still dozens of treaties providing for ICJ dispute resolution as to disputes concerning the interpretation of individual treaties. See Thomas M. Franck, Judging the World Court, at 27–33 (1982).

42 See A. Mark Weisbrud, Failings of the International Court of Justice (2016) (detailed critique of many decisions) and Murphy, supra, at 68–75.

43 Cf., e.g., Gross, supra, at 281–317 (reviewing proposals by International Law Association and others re improving qualifications of judges, expediting proceedings, creating a "preliminary decision procedure" to resolve international law questions in other courts, etc.); Anthony D'Amato, "Modifying U.S. Acceptance of the Compulsory Jurisdiction of the World Court," 79 *Am. J. Int'l L.* 385, 404 (1985) (recommending lifetime tenure and higher salaries); Posner, supra, at 149 (concluding that the ICJ has "done little more than offer a modest alternative to interstate arbitration");

and Franck, supra, Chapters 5 and 6 (somewhat less pessimistic assessment, but still ends up suggesting only a modest role for ICJ regarding issues not relating to the use of force).

44 Oscar Schachter, International Law: Theory and Practice, at 218 (1991).

45 Oscar Schachter, "In Defense of International Rules on the Use of Force," 53 *U. Chi. L. Rev.* 113, 144 (1986). Cf. also Richard B. Bilder, "Some Limitations of Adjudication as an International Dispute Settlement Technique," Chapter 1 in Thomas E. Carbonneau, ed., Resolving Transnational Disputes through International Arbitration (1984). But cf. Oscar Schachter, "Dispute Settlement and Countermeasures in the International Law Commission," 88 AJIL 471, 476 (1994) (much more sympathetic view toward ADR).

46 Julius Stone, Of Law and Nations: Between Power Politics and Human Hopes, at 19 n. 12 (1974).

47 Id. at 107–108.

48 Id. at 214–217.

49 Id. at 445. Professor Stone avers that the Soviet Union, in particular, would never agree since their then doctrine of "liberation of peoples" required the disregard of international law. Id. at 446. As will be seen, he was wrong about this, as Mikhail Gorbachev did agree in principle to the compulsory jurisdiction of the ICJ. See note 55 infra.

50 Richard A. Falk, "The Adequacy of Contemporary Theories of International Law: Gaps in Legal Thinking," 50 *Va. L. Rev.* 231, 247 (1964).

51 The synergy may work both ways. The existence of adequate global dispute resolution systems will help eliminate the need for nuclear weapons. Moreover, in order to abolish nuclear weapons, we may find we need to abolish war altogether. Happily, in order to abolish war, the threat provided by nuclear weapons may be just what is needed to do precisely that. See "Einstein on the Atomic Bomb," *Atlantic Monthly*, November 1947: "Since I do not foresee that atomic energy is to be a great boon for a long time, I have to say that for the present it is a menace. Perhaps it is good that it is so. It may intimidate the human race into bringing order into its international affairs, which, without the pressure of fear it would not do" (emphasis added). See also Peace with Justice: Selected Addresses of Dwight D. Eisenhower, at 11 (1961) ("Thus, the possibility of total destruction, terrible though it is, could be a blessing as all nations, great and small, for the first time in human history, are confronted by an inescapable physical proof of their common lot") (address at Columbia University, March 23, 1950) and Martin Gilbert, A History of the Twentieth Century, at 466 (2001) (Churchill [1953]: "Indeed, I have sometimes the odd thought that the annihilating character of these agencies may bring an utterly unforeseeable security to mankind").

52 See, e.g., Alexander K. Bollfrass, "Governance of a Nuclear Disarmament Treaty," Chapter 7 in Barry M. Blechman & Alexander K. Bollfrass, eds., Elements of a Nuclear Disarmament Treaty (2010).

53 Article 40 of the Charter provides that the Security Council may "to prevent an aggravation of the situation…call upon the parties concerned to comply with such provisional measures as it deems necessary or desirable." Instead of this provision never being used (to my knowledge and that of two experts on the UN it has never been used in the past 30 years),

there is no reason it could not frequently be used, becoming a habit, i.e., a customary norm. We cannot know how the idea of international dispute resolution will eventually be effectuated. The main thing is that the idea itself becomes common and accepted.

54 Louis B. Sohn, "International Arbitration in Historical Perspective," in A.H.A. Soons, ed., International Arbitration: Past and Prospects, at 72 (1990).

55 See Barbara Walker, ed., Uniting the Peoples and Nations, at 234 (1993) (quoting Gorbachev's speech of September 17, 1987: "Its [the ICJ's] man-datory jurisdiction should be organized by all on mutually agreed-upon conditions. We are convinced that a comprehensive system of security is, at the same time, a system of universal law and order ensuring the primacy of international law in politics"). See also Richard B. Bilder, "Judicial Procedures Relating to the Use of Force," Chapter 28 in Lori Fisler Damrosch & David J. Scheffer, Law and Force in the New International Order (1991) (Gorbachev proposed expanding ICJ's com-pulsory jurisdiction, discussions taking place amongst the P-5 for several years) and Ian Brownlie, "Arbitration and International Adjudication: Comments on a Paper by Judge M. Lachs," at 57 n. 5, in A.H.A. Soons, ed., International Arbitration: Past and Prospects (1990) (English text published in *Soviet News* [London] and referred to in only one British newspaper and no American newspapers).

56 Of course, Gorbachev has been replaced by Vladimir Putin, an increas-ingly paranoid autocrat. Cf. Richard Lourie, Putin: His Downfall and Russia's Coming Crash (2017). But Putin will not be there forever, and the fact that compulsory jurisdiction was agreed to once suggests that it could happen again. See Chapter 12 infra at nn. 17, 18, 42, 43, 45(possibility of change in Russia).

57 See Mark W. Janis, An Introduction to International Law, at 74 (4th ed. 2003) ("there is no doubt that international judges and arbitrators can be given explicit equitable powers to supplement or modify international law rules").

58 See David D. Caron, "War and International Adjudication: Reflections on the 1899 Peace Conference," 94 *Am J. Int'l Law* 4, 8 (2000) ("there may be limits" to an international court's ability to render reasoned judgments on some issues) and Milton Katz, The Relevance of International Adjudica-tion, Chapter 2 (1968).

59 International courts tend to be especially concerned about this issue, given the fragility of the entire international law enterprise. See, e.g., Daniel Terris, Cesare P.R. Romano, & Leigh Swigart, The International Judge: An Introduction to the Men and Women Who Decide the World's Cases, Chapter 4 (2007).

60 Cf. Melanie E. Greenberg, John H. Barton, & Margaret McGuiness, eds., Words Over War: Mediation and Arbitration to Prevent Deadly Conflict, at 30–33, 287–288, 357–360, 368 (2000) (existing international law not always helpful in resolving international conflicts).

Special procedural arrangements, such as expert panels or commis-sions, could be used to handle cases that raise primarily "non-legal" or mixed claims. Of course, the availability of international dispute resolution systems would not preclude resort to a variety of "legislative" or diplomatic initiatives. See, e.g., Bill Hayton, The South China Sea: The Struggle for Power in Asia, at 243 (2014) (an example of marine conservation park idea).

61 This would have the additional advantage of eliminating the "gaps" and "fragmentation" problems that have so troubled international legal scholars for decades.

62 See Louis B. Sohn, "The Role of Arbitration in Recent International Multilateral Treaties," in Thomas E. Carbonneau, ed., Resolving Transnational Disputes Through International Arbitration, at 38 (1984).

63 Among the questions that would need to be addressed: Should the ICJ have certain kinds of "appellate" jurisdiction? See, e.g., Francisco Orrego Vicuna, International Dispute Settlement in an Evolving Global Society: Constitutionalization, Accessibility, Privatization, at 120–122 (2004) (appeals of arbitrations); Cesare P.R. Romano, "The United States and International Courts: Getting the Cost-Benefit Analysis Right," at 424 n. 17, in Romano, ed., The Sword and the Scales: The United States and International Courts and Tribunals (2009) (same); and Charney, supra at 71–81 (pros and cons as to other forms of appellate review). What should the scope of appellate review be as to arbitrations? Should it be subject to agreement in advance by the parties? Should there be appellate review of the WTO and the LOS tribunals? How are fact disputes to be resolved? See Anna Riddell & Brendan Plant, Evidence Before the International Court of Justice (2009).

64 See, e.g., Charles S. Rhyne, International Law: The Substance, Processes, Procedures and Institutions for World Peace with Justice, at 252–257, 260–264 (1971); Charney, supra, at 76 (disputants may be more comfortable with persons attuned to their culture); and J.G. Merrills, International Dispute Settlement, Chapter 11 (5th ed. 2011) (the role of regional organization in dispute resolution more generally).

65 See, e.g., Rhyne, at 249–252 (1965 World Peace Through Law Center proposal for "lower level disputes" court).

66 See, e.g., Franck, supra, at 72–73 and Merrills, supra, at 137–141. Some additional mechanisms of "fact-finding," such as special masters or commissions of inquiry, may be necessary.

67 See, e.g., Merrills, supra, at 44–47, 50, 55, 65–69, 72–73, 75–78 (wide array of variations, e.g., some "inquiry" proceedings can resemble arbitration; use of administrative tribunals similar to arbitration; "institutionalized negotiation"; "quasi-arbitration"; and "compulsory conciliation" at parties' option) and Vicuna, supra, at 107–123 (highlighting, e.g., flexible mediation techniques, a wide variety of arbitration rules in use, including expedited procedures, various "combined" approaches, such as mediation followed by arbitration).

68 Although some existing mechanisms could be used to enforce compliance, new ones such as this may need to be created.

69 Cf. Harold Hongju Koh, "How Is International Human Rights Law Enforced?," 74 *Ind. L.J.* 1397, 1407 (1999) ("As always, the best way to enforce legal norms is not to coerce action, not to impose sanctions, but to change the way people think…to internalize rules….").

70 See Jonathan Granoff, "Draft Proposal for the Creation of United Nations Centers for Nonviolent Conflict Prevention," Global Security Institute

Policy Brief (November, 2012) and David A. Hamburg, No More Killing Fields: Preventing Deadly Conflict, at 80–82, 125–126, 229–235 (2002).

71 See, e.g., Ian Kearns, "Avoiding War in Europe: The Risks from NATO-Russian Close Military Encounters," *Arms Control Today*, v. 45, no. 9, pp. 8–13 (need to expand existing agreements on avoiding accidents to Euro-Atlantic area, or possibly worldwide).

72 Which would have expanded jurisdiction covering the future crimes of possession of nuclear weapons or their components.

73 Although the world is probably not yet ready for such an institution, see Stefan Trechsel, "A World Court for Human Rights?," 1 *NW U. J. Int'l Human Rights* 3 (2004), a project is underway to create a new World Court of Human Rights, cf. www.worldcourtofhumanrights.net. Perhaps more likely of adoption would be giving the ICJ a discretionary review of decisions of regional human rights courts.

74 Brian Urquhart, "The Outlaw World," *New York Review of Books*, May 11, 2006, at 25.

10 A United Nations peace force

An international police force, a United Nations Peace Force (UNPF), would be capable of performing several key functions: (1) as an enforcement arm for an international dispute resolution system; (2) to deter international (and perhaps other) violence; and (3) as a substitute, to a considerable extent, for individual country armed forces.[1] As we have seen, several prominent figures have endorsed this basic idea over the years, including at least four American presidents: Theodore Roosevelt, William Howard Taft, Dwight D. Eisenhower, and John F. Kennedy.

Other prominent peace activists are in agreement. In particular, Professor Randall Forsberg (1943–2007), who was Director of the Institute for Defense and Disarmament Studies at MIT, Co-Founder of the Nuclear Weapons Freeze Campaign, recipient of a MacArthur Foundation "genius" award, and probably the best strategic thinker in the American peace movement in the past several decades, dealt specifically with the pacifist position that war is always wrong and that there are no morally acceptable military forces, as follows:

> Others believe with equal conviction, as I do, that complete renunciation of the use of armed force in all situations is much less likely to lead to world peace than is the establishment of an international counterpart to national governments—a reformed U.N. which is empowered to use armed force to deter and quell deadly force.[2]

Forsberg outlines the international structures that would need to be put in place:

> The rule of law must be preeminent. Secondly, there could be vastly strengthened means of nonmilitary conflict resolution … Finally, on the military side there needs to be a process by which reliance on national force … is replaced by reliance on multinational forces.[3]

Professor Forsberg envisioned a ten-year "transitional regime" during which "we can practice sharing power while we still maintain our own unilateral military power or our legal right to use power unilaterally."[4]

One thing upon which peace activists (and others) are agreed is the inadequacy of the current UN system of so-called "collective security."[5] The chief problem has been the veto in the UN's decisive security organ, the Security Council. FDR was very aware of this problem. Back in 1923, when he was a private citizen (between stints as Assistant Secretary of the Navy [1913–1920] and Governor of New York [1929–1932]), he wrote an essay intended to be submitted in an essay contest sponsored by the Saturday Evening Post. He withdrew the essay upon learning that his wife Eleanor would be one of the judges. In the draft essay, he called for the elimination of the unanimity requirement of the then League of Nations, writing: "Common sense cannot defend a procedure by which one or two recalcitrant nations could block the will of the great majority."[6] But in the end, in 1945, the UN did only marginally better than the League, giving the Permanent Five (US, USSR, China, Great Britain and France) a veto in the Security Council. The question for us today is whether we can do any better than that, realizing on the one hand the extreme reluctance of the P-5 to give up or modify their veto powers and, on the other hand, the keen sense of urgency felt by many scholars of national security and, as we've seen, U.S. presidents about the need for some kind of global security force to preserve the peace. The answer to this question may depend upon an answer to the issue of "command and control" over any such force.

A distinguished elder statesman, Elihu Root,[7] noted the difficulties involved in a letter to Charles Francis Adams on February 11, 1915:

> In order that the judgments of the court applying this [international] law shall be respected, there must be sanctions for its enforcement, and here we come to the international police force … Close, discriminating and instructed thought ought to deal with that subject … It is going to be a business for experts who combine technical knowledge with imagination[8]

In other words, it will not be easy. In fact, many if not most commentators of the current generation have viewed it as downright impossible. As usual, the strongest statement of this sort is Eric Posner's:

> Such an [enforcement] agency would need an army or police force armed with guns, and if it would be effective against powerful states, the agency itself would have to have a powerful army. But

what would prevent that agency from using its power to obtain geopolitical ends of its own—or those of its staff or whoever controls it, including, possibly, influential other countries? The answer is—nothing. And that is why a real international enforcement agency does not exist.[9]

And it is true that unless all the major countries were comfortable with the "agency" controlling an international police force, it would never come into being. But are there circumstances under which the major powers would feel comfortable ceding such potentially far-reaching power to some such international agency?

There is, to my knowledge, only one book that systematically addresses this precise question, a remarkable little book edited by Professor Lincoln P. Bloomfield[10] titled "International Military Forces: The Question of Peacekeeping in an Armed and Disarming World" (1964). Professor Bloomfield pulled together eight authors of somewhat varying views for an excellent dialogue on the above question. The book starts with a short history of the idea of an international police force, beginning with Theodore Roosevelt's testimony before Congress[11] regarding a 1910 proposal to create a commission to study "constituting the combined navies of the world [into] an international force for the preservation of universal peace" in connection with arms limitations.[12] Next, there is a post-WWI French proposal for some kind of joint military force under an international general staff, and proposals at the Dumbarton Oaks Conference (1944) by the Soviet Union and China for an international air force.[13] Finally, in 1960 Secretary of State Christian Herter responded to Soviet Premier Khrushchev's call for general and complete disarmament with a proposal for an international force to accompany disarmament.[14]

Although Professor Bloomfield's own concededly "modest" proposal for an international police force is based upon a "generalized sense of short-run caution verging on pessimism," he simultaneously has "a sense of greater optimism for the longer run."[15] In the near term, however, looking at the world in 1964, he believes that (1) it is "surely unsafe to make the ... assumption that the ideological and power struggle between communism and the West will not continue indefinitely,"[16] (2) an effective world police would have to consist of "at least 500,000 men" and "control a nuclear force" of significant size;[17] and (3) none of the superpowers will want to relinquish their veto power.[18]

But if Bloomfield is moderately pessimistic about the idea of a superintending type of international police force, several of his cohorts—in particular, Hans Morgenthau,[19] Stanley Hoffman,[20] and Thomas Schelling[21]—raise a host of very serious objections to the idea.

At the outset, the authors acknowledge that "[a] totally disarmed world is something we know nothing about."[22] As put most evocatively by Thomas Schelling:

> But no one can say in advance whether those who enjoy political control of the force will have the resolve, temerity, prudence, audacity, restraint, brutality, responsibility, or whatever else it takes, to launch war when they ought to, to threaten it credibly, to limit war properly if it occurs, or to abstain in the face of temptation.[23]

And so, the intrepid authors are inevitably forced to speculate, and given when this book was written (1964), while still in the very midst of the Cold War, they do rather well overall.

First, they recognize that a range of different kinds of international police forces can be imagined, from existing types to regional forces to a standing fighting force.[24] Similarly, a variety of missions can be imagined.[25] So their recommendations, while often general, also occasionally distinguish out certain missions.

One objection to the general idea of an international police force concerns the reliability of the soldiers making up the force. Morgenthau concludes:

> [I]t is too much to expect that large masses of individual members of different nations could so transfer their loyalties that they would execute reliably and without question whatever orders the international organization might give them.
>
> ...
>
> [Thus], an international police force ... is ... always threatened with partial or total disintegration.[26]

Similarly, Schelling has, as usual, a rather cute way to put much the same concern:

> The capacity to incur allegiance to an abstract organization, or even to "mankind" generally, may not be a capacity highly correlated with other qualities we want in our senior military officers or even our junior ones.[27]

Hoffman concludes that:

> An international standing army is out of the picture. Problems of composition and stationing would be insoluble, and the question of loyalty would arise in its most acute form ... It is impossible to see how today's contenders [nations] would agree on creating such a monster ... What would be the reliability of a force in which totalitarians and non-totalitarians may be juxtaposed, or, if it were drawn exclusively from the reservoir of small, nonaligned states, in which an insidious battle for control would be just as permanent as the army?[28]

A second basic concern, already reflected to some extent in the first, but nevertheless separable is that the East-West divide makes impossible any kind of international police force. Stanley Hoffman makes the point quite forcefully:

> A world force that would be above and beyond the very real lines of enmity that crisscross the world is inconceivable ... The circumstances which doomed Chapter VII [of the UN Charter] have not been transcended ... As long as the major powers are engaged in a contest that may hopefully remain peaceful but is nevertheless total in the sense of being an ideological competition as well as a power struggle, they are unlikely to set up a force which none of them could be sure to control ...[29]

Hoffman does later note, however, that "a passage to a more moderate international system," and at a minimum, the end of the Cold War, might improve the prospects of some kind of international force, e.g., to police arms control agreements.[30]

Third, and really the most important concern, is the critical "command and control" issue: by what process and by whose decision, is an international force to be set in motion? Morgenthau, Hoffman, and Schelling rightly perceive that the answer depends upon what stage of disarmament, if any, has been reached. For Morgenthau, the idea of an international police force in a world of armed or even partially armed sovereign states is "a contradiction in terms," an impossibility.[31] And total disarmament would require "a supranational authority capable of committing organized force," in other words, "world government."[32]

Hoffman similarly argues that there are only two basic models for the international system, either a system of sovereign competing units or a world state.[33] Any system that aims at disarmament and would settle disputes "establishes in fact, if not in words or in intention, the beginning of a world government."[34] Shy of that, the possibility of interstate war will persist.[35] Even assuming some kind of international force were to be imagined, there would be insuperable "command and control" problems, because one of two things would have to occur, either (1) a case-by-case decision by some entity such as the Security Council, or (2) "a fully worked-out agreement defining in advance and in detail the kinds of circumstances in which the force could be used and the kinds of missions it could perform in each case."[36] As to the former, Hoffman is not optimistic about the chances of agreement, given past history. As to the latter:

> [I]t is easy to predict that either the states would fail to agree on a meaningful definition, both exhaustive and precise enough (just as they have failed to define aggression), or also the agreement on a document would not really settle anything, and in case after case a battle royal would break out around the issue as to whether or not the events fell into one of the slots of the agreement.[37]

Similarly, Thomas Schelling, in the course of dealing with what he calls "organizational," "foreign policy," and "techniques of the force" issues, deals with what are a number of command and control issues.[38] Schelling, like Bloomfield, assumes that an international peace force would have to have an "invulnerable nuclear deterrent"[39] and a considerable armed force (he casually mentions force levels in the millions, a budget perhaps half the American and, just for shock value, the possibility of amphibious or airborne attack on, e.g., the United States!).[40] Continuing in a similar vein, he asks whether the force (or the agency that controls it) can use force to extract the money needed to fund it;[41] whether the force could have "spies" (not just "inspections") and military "secrets"; and what to do if the "enemies" of the force are represented on whatever political entity controls it.[42] To top off these troubling questions, he asks whether a force whose function would be to maintain military supremacy against all potential adversaries would be an irreversibly dangerous arrangement.[43]

There are other objections and concerns, such as the perils of involvement in internal upheavals,[44] the risk that a standing or stand-by force would become (or at least be viewed) as being "an instrument at the service of the status quo,"[45] and a host of dilemmas associated with the use of war to prevent war.[46]

All the above is quite daunting to anyone hopeful of rounding out the "world peace through law" formula with some kind of seemingly logically necessary UN Peace Force. Certainly, Bloomfield and his co-authors are right about one central thing: any attempt in today's world to enforce collective security against a major power is "just about as impossible as the drafters of the [UN] Charter calculated."[47]

Does this mean the end of the whole idea of "world peace through law"? Not necessarily. In fact, not at all. There are two reasons. First, we may find that once we have established a viable and well-accepted set of legal structures that constitute a comprehensive system for resolving international disputes, we may not actually need much "force" to secure compliance. Second, it is possible to carve out well-defined tasks which a UNPF can undertake, which will in practice not suffer from the difficulties envisioned by Bloomfield and his co-authors.

Taking the first point. We have already seen that early WPTL theorists, such as Jeremy Bentham and William Howard Taft, felt that once a nation had committed to international dispute resolution and the case was decided, reliance could be had upon the force of international public opinion. Similarly, an early American peace activist, William Ladd,[48] argued for a "court of nations" to "arbitrate or judge" international disputes voluntarily brought to it, "leaving the functions of the executive [enforcement] with public opinion, 'the queen of the world.'"[49] Ladd believed that:

> [W]here one man obeys the laws for fear of the sword of the magistrate, an hundred obey them through fear of public opinion ... [such that] [t]hough at the commencement of this [Court of Nations] system, its success may not be so great as is desirable, yet, as moral power is every day increasing in a geometrical ratio, it will finally take the place of all wars ... much in the same manner as a civil court has taken the place of the judicial combat.[50]

Of course, such pietistic hopes could well be viewed as mere wishful thinking in the face of events such as WWI and WWII and more recent and ongoing wars. Nevertheless, despite the limited role that international law has been allowed to play in the past, it is probably true, as modern scholars of international law point out, that:

> [W]orld public opinion is emerging as one of the most important sanctions in international relations that states must reckon with. As knowledge of international law and acceptance of it grows, public opinion will strengthen the effect of the "Moral Sanction" incurred by the violation of international law.[51]

An interesting feature of European Union law is the enforcement mechanism for judgments of the European Court of Human Rights. There is no compulsory machinery comparable to domestic courts, only Article 53 of the Convention, which provides simply: "The High Contracting Parties undertake to abide by the decision of the Court in any case to which they are parties."[52] Think more generally about the European Union. Was it a supranational police force that made the EU a success? No. It was an agreement to agree that did it. Nor was it, by the way, any one institutional arrangement, agreed upon in advance, such as a parliament, that did it either. Mostly, it all depended ultimately upon a certain attitude, a willingness to follow certain basic rules and norms. As stated by Arthur Larson:

> [I]t cannot be stressed too often that the heart of the matter is not force; it is law. Too often it is assumed that, if we could only create a decisively powerful international police force under central control, the problem of achieving world order would be largely solved. This puts the cart before the horse. The most important thing is to develop a body of law and a machinery of law that all nations accept and trust. To the extent that this can be achieved, history has shown that exacting compliance by force will not ordinarily be necessary.[53]

In sum, if we are ever able to erect a comprehensive set of legal structures at the international level which nations trust to resolve international conflict, we will have accomplished something tremendously significant and valuable all by itself, regardless of enforcement provisions.

What could a UNPF contribute toward peace, keeping in mind the concerns of the skeptics so fully explicated above?

1   **Enforcing international court judgments** First, a UNPF could enforce decisions of the International Court of Justice and other international courts, pursuant to the UN Charter.[54] Although such enforcement would, under existing law, only be discretionary with the Security Council, the record of enforcement is not really so bad thus far,[55] and it is perhaps not wishful thinking to expect an improved record in the future, as well as a discontinuance of the veto as to, in particular, resolutions to enforce ICJ judgments (as part of a sort of "common law" development, or, in this case, "international norm" development).

2   **Genocide prevention and buttressing nation-building** This is not the place for a full discussion of these topics, even though they do have some fairly obvious security implications. Although a greater role for a UNPF to prevent genocide has long been urged, great caution must be exercised to define very carefully when the new "responsibility to protect" norm mandates intervention.[56] Better intelligence-acquisition in any such operations is required, regardless of the consent of the country involved,[57] in order to avoid mistakes in what are often tumultuous and confusing circumstances of civil war or ethnic strife with conflicting claims made by all sides.[58]

    Despite the opposition of a recent American president, the use of UN troops to assist nation-building is something that obviously should have happened much earlier in Iraq and Afghanistan, now costing the U.S. trillions of dollars, thousands of lives, and gaining us nothing but the contempt of a large segment of the world.[59]

3   **The "World Policeman" role** There will of course be many issues as to the precise role a UNPF could play as world policeman. A robust UNPF might be very appropriate for combatting terrorism, especially where it is unclear whose responsibility it is to step in. A huge issue will be whether a UNPF ought to have access to drones and if so when they should be used.[60]

    In addition to the usual Chapter VII discretionary actions, there need to be well-defined circumstances under which a UNPF would be authorized in advance to engage in "virtually automatic action,"[61] much in the way that municipal police respond to a jewelry store burglar alarm. For instance, as noted earlier, it would be an international crime to possess nuclear weapons or their components, and there is no need for the Security Council to debate whether to arrest someone who violates this prohibition.

4   **Enforcing disarmament** Finally, as Stanley Hoffman conceded, once the world frees itself of the intense rivalries of the Cold War and arrives at "a more moderate system," then "at that point arms control agreements could be policed by international forces."[62] Despite recurring turmoil, as argued above, we are gradually heading toward such a more "moderate" world, and perhaps closer than we realize to abolishing nuclear weapons.

The initial question, then, is what kind of UNPF might be needed to enforce a treaty abolishing nuclear weapons? On the one hand, it is conceivable that, depending upon just how "moderate" the world will have become by then, a zero-nukes regime might not require that much "policing" beyond the normal inspections processes, so that one could rely upon current Chapter VII enforcement, which is of course subject to the P-5 veto. On the other hand, if one demands ironclad guaranteed enforcement, then some kind of veto-proof mechanism is required. Is that possible?

Despite ample basis for skepticism about abolishing the P-5 veto in general, there may be some basis for optimism about doing so as to isolated topics. The precedent is the Law of the Sea Treaty, which established adjudicative tribunals that are not subject to any P-5 veto.[63] Similarly, without making premature prescriptions as to what will be a difficult negotiation, some kind of "operational mechanism" to control a UNPF could be created.[64]

What kind of force or forces might we be talking about to enforce a nuclear disarmament treaty? Well, it certainly need not be the millions talked about by some commentators, nor need it (or should it) have nuclear weapons. In fact, it is very possible that the vast majority of actions would be against an individual or a very few individuals, and not entire nations, such that a UNPF could be quite small. But in view of the world as it is, in which the United States spends more on its military than every other country in the world, it is entirely possible that something like an "overgrown NATO" might end up being the default "big army" component of a set of international peace forces.[65]

Finally, what about the problem of "outliers," nations that refuse to abide by a nuclear disarmament treaty? International law must mandate the abolition of nuclear weapons worldwide, and back up this mandate forcefully: to put it bluntly, outliers will be coerced, either politely or impolitely.[66] Possession of nuclear weapons needs to be made an international crime, irrespective of individual state consent.[67] Those who insist on possessing such weapons are threatening to blow up children in their cribs, grandmothers in their rockers, and entire generations of families in an horrific instant. This is a crime against humanity and anyone threatening same is an international outlaw, subject to arrest as such. Careful thought should be given as to precisely how such an arrest might be effectuated in a manner that encourages voluntary compliance and avoids unnecessary bloodshed. But in the end, after exhausting whatever due process mechanisms are devised, a recalcitrant international outlier must be treated in basically the same manner as a domestic murderer.

Not that a UNPF ought to be engaged in nothing but the application of force. On the contrary, there ought to be a "peace and reconciliation" force that makes full use of conflict resolution and other non-violent approaches, something like the existing Non-Violent Peaceforce.[68] There would need to be diverse types of peace forces, appropriately staffed and trained to focus on diverse challenges. Obviously, the UNPFs would need to have a highly-trained corps of elite officers and troops, with access to all necessary weaponry, equipment, logistics, support, and intelligence and communications, operating under well-organized and well-coordinated command and control with clear mandates.[69] Of course, the UN could also utilize existing national forces to operate under UN auspices.

Is general and complete disarmament necessary?

Many, if not most, of the plans for WPTL over the years (e.g., McCloy-Zorin) have contemplated eventual general and complete disarmament (GCD). But is GCD necessary? Even though there is a certain intuitive "logic" behind the idea of a truly "supranational UNPF,"[70] in practice all that may really be needed is (1) acceptance of the rule of law to resolve international conflicts, and (2) an accepted norm of reliance upon a UNPF, such that a UNPF is considered the only legitimate means of confronting violence or threats of violence. In short, under our version of "world peace through law," neither a global legislature nor general and complete disarmament is necessary.[71]

Future directions

The fact that the idea of a robust UNPF might be acceptable to certain conservatives[72] does not necessarily make it a bad idea. Unless some of the ideas of the peace movement are taken up by the so-called "opposition," they will never go anywhere.

In sum, as we every day gain greater experience with already-existing UN peace forces, increasing their capacity and competence, with concomitant probable decreases in individual-country militaries, we will arrive at a point where the normal expectation will be that an international peace force is the only proper means of dealing with international conflict. Simultaneously, the universal expectation and eventual well-settled norm will become that such conflict should be subjected to a comprehensive array of international dispute resolution mechanisms. When that happens, we will have arrived at a place where we have in fact substituted the rule of law for the use of force to resolve international conflict. If and when, that day comes, we will have realized humanity's long-time dream of world peace through law.

Notes

1 The precise extent to which such substitution occurs will depend upon what agreement is negotiated as to conventional arms reductions as part of the abolition treaty. See Chapter 8 supra at note 33. Cf. also discussion at nn. 70–72 infra (general and complete disarmament unnecessary).

2 Elise Boulding & Randall Forsberg, Abolishing War, at 14 (1998). See also
   Hugo Grotius, De Jure Belli ac Pacis Libri Tres, at 20 (Kelsey transl., 1913)
   ("[M]any men … have come to the point of forbidding all use of arms
   to the Christian … [Such men have as their purpose that] when things
   have gone in one direction [following Thirty Years War], to force them in
   the opposite direction, as we are accustomed to do, that they may come
   back to a true middle ground. But the very effort of pressing too hard
   in the opposite direction is often so far from being helpful that it does
   harm, because in such arguments the detection of what is extreme is easy,
   and results in weakening the influence of other statements which are well
   within the bounds of truth. For both extremes, therefore a remedy must
   be found that men may not believe either that nothing is allowable, or that
   everything is.") (emphasis added).
3 Id. at 57.
4 Id. at 59. Cf. id. at 67–68 (eventual transition to standing UN peace
   force). See also James T. Ranney, "Beyond Minimal Deterrence—An
   Approach to Nuclear Disarmament," 4 *J. of World Peace* 18, 19–20
   (Spring, 1987).
5 See, e.g., Thomas M. Franck, Nation against Nation: What Happened to the
   U.N. Dream and What the U.S. Can Do about It, at 62 (1985) ("the U.N.'s
   collective-security machinery has been exposed as absurdly inadequate.").
   Cf. id. at 51 ("There is no collective-security to be had from the U.N.").
6 Townsend Hoopes & Douglas Brinkley, FDR and the Creation of the
   U.N., at 11 (1997).
7 Secretary of War, 1899–1904; Secretary of State, 1905–1909; U.S. Senator,
   1909–1915; President of Carnegie Foundation, 1910–1925.
8 Philip C. Jessup, Elihu Root, at 373 (1938).
9 Eric A. Posner, The Perils of Global Legalism, at 32 (2009).
10 Professor of Political Science Emeritus, MIT. He has three degrees from
   Harvard, 4 years in the US Navy, and 11 years at the State Department.
   He was Director of Global Issues on the NSC staff.
11 Like everyone else, Professor Bloomfield fails to note Roosevelt's 1910
   Nobel speech.
12 Bloomfield, at 5.
13 Id. There were, of course, the provisions of the UN Charter for mere
   collective security (Chapter VII), but nothing approaching an international
   police force came of this due to the Cold War. Id. at 6–7.
14 Id. at 4 (the author editorializes that this revolutionary idea "was
   advanced, one suspects, without full comprehension of its implications").
   Cf. id. at 11–15 (similar discussion of 1961 McCloy-Zorin Accord).
15 Id, at vi.
16 Id. at 19. See id. at 38, 57–58.
17 Id. at 16. See id. at 18 (even after disarmament, international police would
   have to retain nuclear weapons to guard against clandestine production).
   But see Chapter 10 infra (no such thing contemplated).
18 Id. at 19.
19 Hans Morgenthau (1904–1980) was one of the founders of the Political
   Realism school of thought. For decades, his 1948 book, "Politics among
   Nations," which went through many editions, was the most widely used text
   in international relations courses. See generally William E. Scheuerman,
   Hans Morgenthau: Realism and Beyond (2009).

20 Stanley Hoffman (1925–2010) was a Harvard professor who, happily, is not easily pigeon-holed. He was a brilliant critic of the Iraq war and of calling Iran part of "the axis of evil" (on the obvious ground that this gave a big boost to the forces of reaction in Iran). Cf. www.discoverthenetworks. org/printindividualProfile,asp?indid=1590.

21 Thomas Schelling (1921–2016) was a professor of public policy, University of Maryland College Park. He authored "Arms and Influence" (1966), an extremely influential book on nuclear strategy.

22 Hoffman, in International Military Forces, at 188. See id. (Bloomfield) at 4: "As one tackles the several meanings of 'international force' it is striking how little experience the world has actually had that could illuminate the future."). Cf. id. (Schelling) at 213–214 ("We do not know whether an international military organization would have independent financial means of support, secure access to supplies, and its own intelligence service.").

23 Id. at 235.

24 Id. at 8.

25 Id. at 9–10 (e.g., observation, enforcing ceasefires, and actual combat).

26 Id. at 178–179.

27 Id. at 230.

28 Id. at 200–201. Hoffman concedes only that: "A permanent standing army may be conceivable in a post-nationalist age when world politics would be much more moderate than in the past century."

29 Id. at 198–199. As for "a force established by a coalition composed of one major power, its allies, and the bulk of the 'nonaligned' states [that] would be a kind of NATO force writ large ... [it] would all too easily be denounced as a recipe for world war." Id. at 199–200.

30 Id. at 208, 209–210.

31 Id. at 181, 182.

32 Id. at 182. Which he does not even bother to say is also impossible. For similar modern views, cf. Douglas J. Feith & Abram Shulsky, "The Dangerous Illusion of 'Nuclear Zero'" (Hudson Institute), www.educationnews.org/ ed_reports/thinks_tanks/91661.html?print.

33 Id. at 189.

34 Id.

35 Id. at 189–190.

36 Id. at 202.

37 Id.

38 In an early footnote, he notes that the whole issue of how an international police force would fit into some larger organization is not addressed, including whether there would be some parliamentary body, some executive body (military or civilian), or some executive-administrative body above the armed forces. Id. at 214 n. 1.

39 Id. at 214.

40 Id. at 214–215.

41 Id. at 216.

42 Id. at 218–220.

43 Id. at 224.

44 Cf. id. at 207 (Hoffman).

45 Id. at 200 (Hoffman).

46 Cf. id. at 225–226, 228 (Schelling).

47 Id. at 205 (Hoffman). Cf. also id. at 233 (Schelling): "it is unlikely that an international strategic command would have a completely reliable, credible capability to intervene and to stop any rearmament of a major industrial power."

48 1778–1841; Harvard graduate [1797]; sailor; farmer; and peace activist.

49 William Ladd, An Essay on a Congress of Nations for the Adjustment of International Disputes without Resort to Arms, at xlix–l (1840; Carnegie reprint, 1916).

50 Id. at 6–7.

51 Charles S. Rhyne, International Law: The Substance, Processes, Procedures and Institutions for World Peace with Justice, at 9 (1971). See also Harold Hongju Koh, "Why Do Nations Obey International Laws?," 106 Yale L.J.2599, 2645 (1997) (voluntary compliance, due to perception of law's fairness, the way most legal systems work) and Tad Daley, Apocalypse Never: Forging the Path to a Nuclear Weapons-Free World, at 192–94 (2010) (world opinion is what has deterred use of nuclear weapons since 1945).

52 Cited in Mark W. Janis, An Introduction to International Law, at 267 (3rd ed. 1999).

53 Arthur Larson, When Nations Disagree, at 217 (1961) (emphases added). Cf. id.: "Moreover, only as this is achieved will nations lay down their arms, since the only force that can fill the vacuum created by the removal of armaments is the rule of law." Cf. also id. at 195 (explaining historical record of compliance with international law rulings, because once nations have submitted to an international tribunal "they are by then 'in so deep' that it becomes unthinkable to refuse compliance when the decision has been rendered.").

54 Article 94(2), UN Charter (Security Council has discretion "to decide upon measures to be taken to give effect to the judgment."). Of course, such measures could be less intrusive than a UNPF.

55 Even in *Nicaragua v. United States*, the U.S. eventually settled. See O'Connell, supra, at 299 n.17.

56 Under Arts. 2(4) & (7), UN Charter, R2P cannot operate in the face of a Security Council veto. While a kind of common law "overlay" might be said to guide exercise of said veto power, what is ultimately needed is an amendment of Art. 51 to permit "defense of others" in carefully defined circumstances (analogous to domestic criminal law). Cf. generally Robert C. Johansen, ed., A United Nations Emergency Peace Service to Prevent Genocide and Crimes Against Humanity (2006) and Sarah Sewell, Dwight Raymond, & Sally Chin, Mass Atrocity Response Operations: A Military Planning Handbook (2010) (Carr Center at Harvard working with Army War College to create first military manual re how to enforce R2P).

57 See Samantha Power, "A Problem from Hell": America and the Age of Genocide, at 340–341 (2002) (Canadian Major General Romeo Dallaire, commander of UN peacekeeping forces in Rwanda, suffered from abysmal lack of intelligence and institutional support; the tiny UN Department of Peacekeeping Operations, with a staff of a few hundred, is responsible for 70,000 peacekeepers) and Brian E. Urquhart, in Bloomfield, ed., supra, International Military Forces, at 141.

58 See, e.g., "The Perils of Peacekeeping," *The Economist*, August 14, 2010, at 37–37 (impossible or difficult claims to reconcile) and "Revisiting the killing fields," *The Economist*, September 4, 2010, at 51–52 (counter-genocide to Rwandan genocide).

59 See, e.g., Joseph E. Stiglitz & Linda J. Bilmes, The Three Trillion Dollar War: The True Cost of the Iraq Conflict (2008) and Steve Chapman, "The real cost of endless war," *The Week*, August 20, 2010, at 14 (Bilmes reports that costs are outpacing original estimates "and could eventually reach $8 trillion"). Cf. generally Joris Voorhoeve, From War to Rule of Law: Peacebuilding after Violent Conflicts (2004).

60 Cf. David Cole, "The Drone Presidency," *New York Review of Books*, August 18, 2016, at 21 (need for international standard for use of drones).

61 See Arthur Larson, When Nations Disagree, at 215–216.

62 Hoffman, in Bloomfield, supra, at 209–210.

63 Cf. discussion supra in Chapter 7 at note 18.

64 Nevertheless, for the sole purpose of showing that some formula could be devised, one could postulate the possibility of some combination of (a) qualified majority voting and (b) weighted voting, with no one country having more than a certain percentage of the vote. Cf. generally as to weighted voting schemes, Joseph Schwartzberg, Transforming the United Nations System: Designs for a Workable World (2013).

65 See Lincoln P. Bloomfield, International Military Forces: The Question of Peacekeeping in an Armed and Disarming World, at 97 n. 16 (1964) (already speculations along these lines in 1963); Christoph Marischka, "How Ban Ki-moon subjugated the UN to NATO," *Informationsstelle Militarisierung*, June 1, 2009 (www.imi-online.de/2009.php3?id+1925) (largely unnoticed document of 23 September 2008 signals cooperation between UN and NATO); Lawrence S. Kaplan, NATO and the UN: A Peculiar Relationship (2010); and Editorial, "Why NATO?," *The Nation*, May 28, 2012, at 3 ("In theory, a NATO that pooled Europe's and America's political and military resources and acted only on UN Security Council authorization could be a useful part of the world's security architecture."); and Gen. Tony Zinni & Tony Koltz, Before the First Shots Are Fired: How America Can Win or Lose Off the Battlefield, at 161 (2014).

66 See Jonathan Schell, The Gift of Time, supra, at 204–205 (retired General George Lee Butler envisions in such a case an immediate intervention and physical removal of leadership of state, if necessary);Martin Butcher, What Wrongs Our Arms May Do: The Role of Nuclear Weapons in Counterproliferation, at 86 (2003) ("The Security Council would, given an international norm against the possession of [nuclear] weapons, seem to have the power to decide that the possession of [nuclear] weapons by any nation is illegal and that action must be taken to remove that capability ... "); and Art. 2(6), UN Charter ("The Organization shall ensure that States which are not Members of the United Nations act in accordance with these Principles as far as may be necessary for the maintenance of peace and security.").

67 See ICJ, Advisory Opinion on the *Reservations to the Convention on the Prevention and Punishment of the Crime of Genocide*, I.C.J. Reports 1951, p. 15, at 23 (May 28, 1951) (humanitarian principles underlying the Convention were "binding on States, even without any conventional obligation.").

68 See www.nonviolencepeaceforce.org.

69 See Mary Kaldor, New & Old Wars: Organized Violence in a Global Era, at 59, 64–66, 124–131 (1999) (need for "robust" UNPF willing and able to

undertake military and police and humanitarian tasks, including capture of war criminals, able "to protect aid convoys or safe havens [instead of being] 'like eunuchs at the orgy'").

70 I was among those thinking so at one time. See James T. Ranney, "Beyond 'Minimal Deterrence'—An Approach to Nuclear Disarmament," 4 *J. of World Peace* 18, 19 (Spring 1987) ("it would seem that, one way or another, a monopoly of all internationally usable military force will be required, and there must be at least a de facto reliance upon international law for resolution of international conflict."). See also FDR's Address to Congress, January 6, 1941: "The fourth [freedom] is freedom from fear—which translated into world terms, means a world with a reduction of armaments to such a point and in such a thorough fashion that no nation will be in a position to commit an act of physical aggression against any neighbor—anywhere in the world."

71 Cf. Jonathan Dean, "Convincing the Nuclear-weapon States to Disarm: The Problem of Conventional Forces," Chapter 4 in Jozef Goldblat, ed., Nuclear Disarmament: Obstacles to Banishing the Bomb, at 50 (2000) ("it would be mistaken to insist that complete conventional disarmament must accompany nuclear disarmament.").

72 Cf. Nina M. Serafino, "The Global Peace Operations Initiative: Background and Issues for Congress" (Congressional Research Service, March 19, 2009) (even the Bush administration favored multilateral peacekeeping and stabilization forces).

11 Objections

Although we have at times treated WPTL as a moderate non-radical proposal, it must be admitted that what WPTL contemplates is a profound change in international security arrangements. Turning away from war and relying instead upon the global rule of law to resolve international conflict will surely be one of the most important events in human history. It is therefore worth taking the time to address possible objections to the overall proposal.

The most obvious objection to our updated version of WPTL is that it is simply impossible because it involves too much interference with national sovereignty, would break down in the face of serious threats of violence, and would not be enforceable if push came to shove.

It is true that significant intrusions upon national sovereignty are contemplated, even though they would be agreed upon, like any other treaty. Thus, the Bully Boys of the world would have to forego the guilty little pleasures they've allowed themselves over the years, such as mining Nicaraguan harbors, the second Iraq War, and Crimea. WPTL will interfere with aggression. Countries contemplating joining a WPTL security regime, which would mandate compulsory international dispute resolution to resolve international conflict, would have to decide whether they are willing to incur a substantial diminution in their sovereignty in order to preserve global security. In the end, predictions in advance, either way, do not count for much. All that will ultimately matter is what countries are eventually willing to do. While right now may seem like the worst of times to expect such an agreement, history demonstrates that it is often precisely such dark times that lead to major social and political change.

World federalists will make a related objection: that a treaty is a mere scrap of paper, that what is required is the "constitution of a world government."[1] But a constitution is nothing more than a glorified treaty. Constitutions, like treaties, are capable of being destroyed by sufficiently determined dissenters, just as the South attempted to do in the American Civil War. In sum, just as there are weak constitutions and strong constitutions, there are weak and strong treaties. We need a strong treaty, one supported by an increasingly strong international norm favoring compulsory international dispute resolution.

While much of WPTL may be objected to as merely "aspirational" in nature, it is submitted that it could also be quite pragmatic and would not break down in the face of severe conflicts. If we try to envision conflicts that could arise in the future that might challenge the feasibility of such an international regime, we can start by looking at some of the major crises and conflicts over the past half century or so, as well as a few pending conflicts, to try to estimate how well WPTL might have worked or would work if "push came to shove."[2]

When we do so, it is surprising how well WPTL works in virtually every case. Starting with WWI, as we've seen, the very first stage of international dispute resolution, compulsory negotiation, would have helped (as opposed to the ultimatum which Austro-Hungary issued to Serbia, which was purposely designed to be unacceptable), if not totally resolved the problem, and other post-WWII legal restraints upon aggression would almost certainly have given the relevant officials of the Austrian government second thoughts.[3]

But what about WWII and Adolf Hitler, a very determined aggressor. Even Hitler, however, was quite worried prior to invading Poland that, as he put it, "some Schweinhund will make a proposal for mediation."[4] Thus, if at the time there had been a well-established norm requiring resort to global dispute resolution mechanisms as well as clear law making aggression illegal, all backed up by a standing UN Peace Force, this might well have made all the difference.

Another very difficult case is the Cuban Missile Crisis. One can start by agreeing with the fundamental assumption held by the Kennedy administration that Soviet nuclear missiles in Cuba were unacceptable, regardless of what "the law" may have had to say about it.[5] Nevertheless, this very case is one where under a regime of zero nuclear weapons, as contemplated under our WPTL proposal, this seemingly "hard case" disappears altogether.

As to pending conflicts, it is amazing how many of the current ones that are occasioning the most urgent talk of war would immediately disappear as sources of conflict under a WPTL regime. Both Iran and North Korea, under a WPTL zero-nukes regime, would be unconditionally prohibited from possessing nuclear weapons. Hence, the major source of concern in regard to these countries would be gone. As noted above, we may be surprised at the extent to which nuclear weapons are themselves a major source of fear and conflict, therefore making us less safe. As to Iran in the near term, whatever reservations some may have as to the Joint Comprehensive Plan of Action,[6] if we are able to secure at least the beginnings of some kind of abolition convention in the next decade, it will have facilitated Iran's adherence to such a convention. As to North Korea, it may be noted at the outset that the very fact that North Korea now possesses nuclear weapons proves the irrationality of the entire nuclear-weapons regime, for if the crazy dictator of a poverty-stricken country can become a nuclear weapons power, then anyone can, which is a frightening fact.[7] As to what should be done next in regard to North Korea, this is an obvious case for compulsory international dispute resolution: rather than debating whether we should even talk with the regime,[8] or considering what would be illegal pre-emptive military strikes,[9] such talks ought to be compulsory.[10]

As to the difficult problems posed by the Palestine/Israel conflict, if it could be made to fit the terms of an alternative dispute resolution treaty signed by both sides, all that can be said is that the WPTL formula is not magic, and there would be no substitute for the kinds of hard work that finally resulted in peace in Northern Ireland.[11]

It is also true that many current conflicts such as the one in Syria, involving many non-state actors, would not fall within the purview of an alternative dispute resolution treaty signed by only nation states. Nevertheless, as we gained greater experience with a WPTL regime, it is likely that elements of the WPTL formula would help provide solutions to even extremely challenging problems such as Syria. Already many commentators are urging the use of an international peace force as part of some kind of multination/multiparty solution.[12] Furthermore, existing elements of the global rule of law, in particular, the International Criminal Court, could play a useful role in resolving the crisis in Syria. If Bashir-al-Assad were indicted for war crimes, this might hasten his removal from office, perhaps in return for the dropping of ICC charges.[13]

As to the ongoing crisis in the Ukraine, this is a perfect case for the application of the mandatory negotiation and mediation approaches, especially when one appreciates the full historical and strategic context and the parties' true interests.[14]

Lastly, as to the many other areas of conflict and potential conflict in the world, such as the South China Sea, here too some form of international dispute resolution is at least one of the obvious answers.[15]

In sum, without going through all past and present conflicts, it seems reasonably clear that (1) virtually all violent confrontations might have been avoided if some form of compulsory dispute resolution had been available;[16] (2) even if one can conceive of a case where WPTL might not have worked, there would have been no harm in attempting to use international dispute resolution techniques; and (3) the fact that WPTL does not directly address "lesser wars" such as civil wars ought not to be held against it as long as it prevents all major war.

In any event, regardless of whether WPTL is capable of meeting every variety of crisis, as Arthur Larson notes:

> The true measure ... of the contribution of the peace through law movement will be found not merely in the number of actual disputes settled in court but also in the general increase in respect for legal rights and procedures and in the general elevation of the standard of international conduct that would flow from the strengthening of the substance and machinery of international law.[17]

We are not yet at that point. We have not backed off from Cold War thinking.[18] The requisite trust needed for the abolition of nuclear weapons and global dispute resolution has not yet been realized. Each nation will need to be prepared to accept an occasional adverse decision, as William Howard Taft and Dwight David Eisenhower have argued.[19]

A second possible objection to our version of WPTL is that it is unnecessary. One version of the argument might be that all that is actually necessary is to abolish nuclear weapons. One response to this is that WPTL may be necessary, at least in some form, in order to get all the way down to global zero.[20] A second obvious response to this objection is that there are still significant dangers of war with conventional weapons, dangers that should be dealt with via the global rule of law.

Another version of this argument would relate to the UNPF, arguing that all we really need for a peaceful and just future world is the classic idea of a gradual but steady decline in militarism and military spending worldwide, as part of a generalized increase in understanding amongst countries (what might be called the "friendly porcupines" model of world peace). For just as we would no longer think of going to war with Canada and just as Great Britain and France would no longer think of going to war, so too we and Russia and others may arrive at a similar point of mutual understanding in our joint destinies. And this new outlook would be accompanied by the de facto resort to readily available legal dispute resolution systems, without much if any need for a UNPF. If true, fine. But in the meantime, it seems advisable to plan for the kinds of UN Peace Forces envisioned, while conceding that maybe twenty to thirty years from now we will live in a less Hobbesian/Thucydidean world than we do now, and the need to use force for law enforcement will be much less.

The third objection to WPTL would be an alleged "democracy deficit" associated with the lack of any plans for a global legislature. There are several responses. First, as we have previously noted, there is no need for a legislature to have a viable global rule of law. The basic common law processes for developing the law—based if necessary upon nothing more than the Golden Rule and Common Sense—is what all early equity courts and indeed all the earliest courts in human history have used[21] and the results have been rather satisfactory. Another response is that our recent experience with "democracy" in this country leaves one wondering about the supposed wondrous efficacy of same.[22] We have seen repeated instances of legislation favored by huge majorities fail miserably in the congress.[23] In sum, in the real world, it would appear that treaties agreed upon by almost all countries are in fact generally more "democratic" (in the most fundamental sense of being supported by the vast majority of the people) than U.S. legislation. The great Chief Justice John Marshal, in a letter to international law scholar Henry Wheaton, said he believed that international law was:

> a law which contributes more to the happiness of the human race, than all the statues which ever came from the hands of the sculptor, or all the paintings that were ever placed on canvas.[24]

A fourth objection would be that the elimination of all war is undesirable, in that some wars are worth fighting. For instance, the First Gulf War in 1990, which was fought to reverse the illegal aggression by Saddam Hussein into Kuwait, was clearly legal under Article 2(4) of the UN Charter, and nothing in a WPTL treaty would change this. Security Council-authorized military actions would be exceptions to the general rule requiring that all international conflicts be subject to international dispute resolution.[25] Relatedly, there may be instances where an emergency military response by the UN Peace Force is necessary, without any intervening conflict resolution, via whatever vote is required to trigger the international peace force. The "global rule of law" concept contemplates, as noted above, simple law enforcement of pre-existing rules.

Finally, it may be objected that there is no guarantee that WPTL will work each and every time as to every possible conflict, which is true. Nothing is a "guarantee" of world peace.[26] In the end, whichever way we turn, whatever course of action (or inaction) we choose, there are risks either way, and we are inevitably forced to weigh the relative risks. When one does that, a course that accords with our most precious human values seems infinitely preferable to one that risks the ultimate human disaster.

Bertrand Russell wrote a great little book in 1959 called "Common Sense and Nuclear Warfare." In it, he proposed nuclear disarmament and creation of a "permanent joint body to seek measures tending toward peace," including "deciding disputes by arbitration or by some international tribunal."[27] And he said this:

> I put first among the gains to be expected [from his proposals] the removal of that terrible load of fear which weighs at present upon all those who are aware of the dangers with which mankind is threatened. I believe that a great upsurge of joy would occur throughout the civilized world and that a great store of energies now turned to hate and destruction and futile rivalry would be diverted into creative channels, bringing happiness and prosperity to parts of the world which, through long ages, have been oppressed by poverty and excessive toil. I believe that the emotions of kindliness, generosity and sympathy, which are now kept within iron fetters by the fear of what enemies may do, would acquire a new life and a new force and a new empire over human behaviour. All this is possible. It needs only that men should permit themselves a life of freedom and hope from which they are now excluded by the domination of unnecessary fear.[28]

We know full well by now man's capacity for evil. But we also know of humanity's demonstrable capacity for good, selfless love and kindliness. We must hope that it is this capacity which prevails.[29]

Notes

1 Mortimer J. Adler, How to Think about War and Peace, at 293 (1944) (emphasis added).
2 Obviously, this is something that trained historians and others would need to do to even begin to have any validity. I am aware of only one author, Arthur Larson, who has attempted a similar analysis. See Larson, When Nations Disagree, supra, at 7–8, 102–115 (selected number of conflicts). While Larson seeks to show that most of these incidents involved "justiciable" questions, under our proposal it would not matter whether the dispute was justiciable or not.
3 Following the 2010 Kampala Accord, we have finally nailed down the definition of "aggression" under international law. The International

Criminal Court and other specialized tribunals have begun to prosecute heads of state for war crimes and the like. See Ellen L. Lutz & Caitlin Reiger, eds., Prosecuting Heads of State (2009).

4 William L. Shirer, The Rise and Fall of the Third Reich: A History of Nazi Germany, at 531 (1959).

5 Although the United States defended the legality of their actions, considerable skepticism has been raised about their arguments. See, e.g., Richard A. Falk, "The Adequacy of Contemporary Theories of International Law Gaps in Legal Thinking," 50 *Va. L. Rev. 231,* 234–235, 250 n. 47, and 259 (1964). Also cf. Oscar Schachter, "In Defense of International Rules on the Use of Force," 53 *U. Chi. L. Rev. 113,* 134 (1986)(by relying on ex-post facto "authorization" by the OAS instead of relying upon self-defense, the U.S. "sought to avoid a reciprocal claim that U.S. missile bases near the Soviet Union were unlawful and justified Soviet armed response."). But cf. Shirley V. Scott & Radhika Withana, "The Relevance of International Law for Foreign Policy Decision-making When National Security Is at Stake: Lessons from the Cuban Missile Crisis," 3 *Chinese JIL* 163 (2004) (even though international law was probably not a decisive factor in the decision to utilize a "defensive quarantine" rationale, the legal arguments did help crystallize a solution).

6 See, e.g., Richard Haass, A World in Disarray: American Foreign Policy and the Crisis of the Old Order, at 130–134 (2017).

7 Experts predict that North Korea could have enough fissile material for 100 warheads by 2020. See Daryl G. Kimball, "Curbing the North Korean Nuclear Threat," *Arms Control Today,* at 3 (April 2017).

8 As the current administration is doing—with itself. Secretary of State Tillerson and Vice President Pence say they are "tired of talking," when this administration has not yet talked with the regime once, whereas Secretary of Defense Mattis and President Trump (with qualifications) are willing to talk.

9 A pre-emptive nuclear or non-nuclear strike would not only be illegal under Art. 2(4), UN Charter, it would be unwise, resulting in at minimum the obliteration of Seoul and massive worldwide radiation.

10 See Kimball, supra (step-by-step negotiation process outlined, starting with a moratorium on further tests in return for smaller or delayed joint military exercises by the United States and South Korea).

11 While a WPTL treaty may not be applicable, Kofi Annan believes that an international peace force "will one day form part of the peace and security solution to the conflict." Kofi Annan, Interventions: A Life in War and Peace, at 280 (2012).

12 See, e.g., Michael E. O'Hanlon & Edward P. Joseph, "Bosnia May Offer Road Map for Syria" (*Brookings,* May 23, 2013) (conclude that "any deal is likely to require, among other things, international peacekeepers and that the world is going to have to start getting used to the idea"); Nancy E. Soderberg, "We are letting Assad win" (*Reuters,* March 12, 2012) (urging intervention by regional coalition of the willing, with Arab League and NATO enforcement, to establish safe zones, with a UN Peace Force taking over once there is a peace to keep); and Jessica Mathews, "Is There an Answer for Syria?," *NY Review of Books,* November 4, 2014, at 4 (despite Assad being a war criminal, ISIS has so disrupted both sides that a new

solution involving a unity government and "some kind of international peacekeeping" force may work).

13 Cf. Cale Davis, Political Considerations in Prosecutorial Discretion at the International Criminal Court (2015); Alexander K.A. Greenawalt, "Justice without Politics: Prosecutorial Discretion and the International Criminal Court," 39 Int'l Law & Politics 583 (2007); and Jingbo Dong, "Prosecutorial Discretion at the International Criminal Court: A Comparative Study," 2 *J. of Politics & Law* 109 (2009).

14 See, e.g., "Faculty Member Kachuyevski, Expert on Ukraine, Explains Country's Unrest," *Arcadia Bulletin* (February 26, 2014) ("optimistic" re negotiated settlement) and Eugene Rumer & Andrew S. Weiss, "The Unraveling of Ukraine," www.carnegieendowment.org/2014/05/14/unraveling-of-ukraine/haut (need for immediate international mediation to prevent situation from spiraling out of control). Cf. generally, Samuel Charap & Timothy J. Colton, Everyone Loses: The Ukraine Crisis and the Ruinous Contest for Post-Soviet Eurasia (2017); Marvin Kalb, Imperial Gamble: Putin, Ukraine, and the New Cold War (2015); and Nicolai N. Petro, "Why Russia and Ukraine Need Each Other," 1 *Russian Politics* 184 (2016). It is worth noting that existing international law is not all that helpful in resolving the crisis in Ukraine. See Simon Chesterman, "Crimean War 2: Ukraine and International Law," www.simonchesterman.com/blog/2014/03-15/crime.

15 See Lucy Reed & Kenneth Wong, "Marine Entitlements in the South China Sea: The Arbitration Between the Philippines and China," 110 *Am. J. of Int'l Law* 746 (2016) (review of the 479-page award in favor of Philippines). See also Bill Hayton, The South China Sea: The Struggle for Power in Asia (2014); Robert D. Kaplan, Asia's Cauldron: The South China Sea and the End of a Stable Pacific (2014); and Robert Beckman, Ian Townsend-Gault, Clive Schofield, Tara Davenport, & Leonardo Bernard, Beyond Territorial Disputes in the South China Sea: Legal Frameworks for the Joint Development of Hydrocarbon Resources (2013) (all three books strongly suggestive of need for broad "equity" approach we favor). Also cf. Dune Lawrence & Wenxin Fan, "Saving the South China Sea," *Bloomberg Businessweek*, December 26, 2016, at 78–83 (Professor John McManus proposes making the Spratly Islands into 6-nation marine park).

16 See also Chapter 9 supra (according to historians, negotiation could have likely prevented WW I and other wars; many wars terminated via mediation; all of America's 19th-century wars could have been avoided by arbitration; USSR willing to accept compulsory adjudication).

17 Larson, supra, at 9.

18 Cf. Tony Zhao, "The U.S.-Russia Nuclear Relationship: A New Cold War?," *Carnegie News* (July 17, 2015) and Angela E. Stent, The Limits of Partnership: U.S.-Russian Relations in the Twenty-First Century (2014).

19 See David H. Burton, ed., William Howard Taft: Essential Writings and Addresses, at 263–264 (2009) ("The treaties of arbitration are not going to accomplish substantial progress unless we enter into them with a willingness and a consciousness that they may involve us in decisions to our detriment. We cannot win every case. Nations are like individuals; they are not always right, even though they think they are, and if arbitration

is to accomplish anything, we must be willing to lose and abide by the loss. If we are to establish real arbitral courts which shall be useful as a permanent method of settling international disputes, we must agree in advance what the jurisdiction of these courts shall be, and then abide by their holding ... and perform the judgments that are made against us.") and Chapter 7 note 14 supra (similar statement by Eisenhower).

20 See Jonathan Schell, The Gift of Time: The Case for Abolishing Nuclear Weapons Now, at 165 (1998) (Mikhail Gorbachev is interviewed: "We will never be able to solve the nuclear question unless at the same time we develop a system of international organizations ... and effective systems of regional security ... [T]he international organization should have certain decision-making powers and mechanisms for enforcement.").

21 In other words, initially, the lord of the manor or the king or some designee had the absolute power to decide a matter (call it a "case" if you like) one way or the other. There was no "precedent." Indeed, contrary to common perception, the principle of *stare decisis* does not even appear in British law until several centuries after the common law began to develop. See Theodore F.T. Plucknett, A Concise History of the Common Law, at 348–350 (5th ed. 1956).

22 See, e.g., Eric Alterman et al., "Kabuki Democracy: Why a Progressive Presidency is Impossible, For Now," *The Nation*, August 30/September 6, 2010, at 11–24 (exploring reasons for federal government's "democratic dysfunction;" "the system is rigged" due to "a corrupt capital culture," with billions spent on lobbying; federal government "has become hopelessly undemocratic, poisoned by corruption" [emphasis added]). Cf. also Jane Mayer, Dark Money and the Hidden History of the Billionaires behind the Rise of the Radical Right (2016) and nn. 423–427 infra (money corrupting our congress).

23 See Chapter 7 at note 23 supra (two-thirds approval of Senate rule re treaties a vestige of slaveholding states, such that 6% of the American public can now block treaties). Cf. also Gail Collins interview, Rachel Maddow Show, September 9, 2010 ("at any given time, 5% of the U.S. population is crazy").

24 Mark W.Janis, An Introduction to International Law, at 48 n. 157 (4th ed. 2003). See also Sarah H. Cleveland, "Our International Constitution," 31 *Yale L.J.* 1, 101–104 (2006) (defending international law against "democracy deficit" claims).

25 See generally, G. William Hopkinson, "Overcoming Diplomatic Inertia and Constraint in the Resolution of Major Conflict," Chapter 3 in Julie Dahlitz, ed., Peaceful Resolution of Major International Disputes (1999).

26 Cf. Jonathan Schell, A Hole in the World: An Unfolding Story of War, Protest and the New American Order, at 28 (2004) ("No plan can reduce the danger by 100%, but an 80% or 90% reduction of risk should be possible.").

27 Bertrand Russell, Common Sense and Nuclear Warfare, at 38, 48 (1959).

28 Id. at 51–52.

29 Many years ago, I attended a peace conference at the University of Montana where a very handsome Native American woman said something like this: "If mankind is good, we will survive; if not, we won't."

12 Conclusion

Benjamin Ferencz, the famous Nuremberg prosecutor who was in charge of the Einsatzgruppen cases, has had a lasting influence on the American peace movement.[1] Now 97 years old, with an amazing long-term perspective on the nature of social change, he says this:

> We live in a world that is just beginning to be put together on an international level, that contains the vital component parts for a more civilized world community. Insofar as we succeed in putting the missing parts in place, the world will be more tranquil. To the extent that we don't have those components, the world will be less peaceful.
>   …
> We are at the beginning of an amazing information revolution, the magnitude of which we cannot even grasp. The potential for changing the way people think is enormous. But it will take time. I don't know if it will be a hundred years or two hundred years or more. There is no such thing as instant revolution or painless revolution, but it can be done. How do I know? Well, I see the trend from all the changes I have witnessed during my lifetime. We are spiraling upward.[2]

Ferencz identifies the potential for significant changes in thinking as the crux of the matter. So what will it take to change people's thinking?

It will take what it always takes—courageous and determined action by individuals in the face of strong opposition—to fight for a world without war. "The mode by which the inevitable comes to pass is effort."[3] Effort on many fronts, not just "the law."

Many paths to peace

In some ways, our heavy emphasis upon and focus upon "world peace through law" creates a potentially misleading impression. For if we ever do secure world peace under law, it will only be as something of a capstone to developments in many other fields of endeavor. Law, after all, is merely public sentiment crystallized. Thus, in a way, this book could equally be captioned World Peace Through Increased Understanding; or World Peace Through Interfaith Dialogue; or World Peace Through Education; or World Peace Through an Egalitarian Revolution; or World Peace Through Trade & Tourism; or World Peace Through Music.[4]

Despite there being a somewhat non-serious tone to some of the above motifs, there is actually a profoundly serious aspect to each one. Although we have focused on "world peace through law" as sort of an ultimate direction that humanity can safely head, a multitude other focuses will be critical. In short, each of us has a role to play. What will be required is all of us pulling together, each at our somewhat differing agendas, with groups such as Mayors for Peace, the Middle Powers Initiative, Global Zero, and the Nuclear Threat Initiative pushing for abolition of nuclear weapons, and American Friends Service Committee and WILPF (Women's International League for Peace and Freedom) pushing their multiple worldwide peace and justice agendas, and the Center for Defense Information (staffed with former military) informing Congress about which weapons systems sought by the Pentagon are unnecessary, and United Nations Association and Citizens for Global Solutions seeking ways to preserve and improve the UN.[5]

But just as there are, no doubt, "many paths to peace," a number of things that we can do collectively and individually, to secure peace, there is also a need for a clear vision of an overarching direction that we might safely head. WPTL provides this, offering an eminently practical agenda for social change in the near term. Neither a world parliament nor general and complete disarmament are necessary. Instead, there is a readier path to peace, spelled out by WPTL proponents for centuries: compulsory international dispute resolution.

Now is the time

WPTL is an eminently do-able task in the lifetimes of many of us. While it is probably true that up until now, e.g., post-WWI, when Wilson rejected the idea, or during the depths of the Cold War, it would not have been possible to adopt compulsory international dispute resolution, developments along two lines suggest that now may finally be the time.

Favorable changes in attitudes

First, most importantly, there are a number of favorable changes in attitudes in relevant areas which have occurred and are occurring. Scholars
have found evidence of a decline in war and the culture of war in recent
decades.[6] This, despite America's recent war in Iraq and the ongoing war
in Afghanistan. Whether this is due to the growth of democracies and
the decline of autocracies[7] or increased trade (the "commercial pacifism"
thesis)[8] or some other set of factors need not detain us. What is important for our purposes is that such a decline in major war and the culture
of war may be a necessary prelude to greater reliance upon the rule of
law. We are also about to witness a dramatically important development
in the evolution of humanity: the abolition of nuclear weapons. This is
something that we simply must do, and, as previously indicated, in a
robustly enforceable way. Once nuclear weapons are no longer viewed
as "military" weapons but as sociopathic systems of absolute evil,[9] and
we eliminate the very last one, we will see a transformation of thinking
about the larger issue of how to secure lasting peace.

Further evidence of changing attitudes is the previously noted recent
(January 4, 2007) editorial in the Wall Street Journal by George P. Shultz,
Henry Kissinger, William J. Perry, and Sam Nunn—two former sec-
retaries of state, a former secretary of defense and a former chairman
of the Senate Armed Services Committee—calling for abolition of
nuclear weapons. Nor were they the first. Obviously, Ronald Reagan
and Mikhail Gorbachev preceded them, at the Reykjavik Summit in
October 1986. And Robert McNamara, Manager of Our Missiles longer
than anybody (from 1961 to 1968), likewise came out in favor of abolition
in 2005.[10] The point is that ideas do matter,[11] and they are changing.

Another significant barometer of how our ideas relating specifically
to national security have been changing are the views over time of
George Kennan (1904–2005), famous diplomat (author of the "contain-
ment doctrine" in 1947) and former Director of Policy Planning in the
State Department.[12] Kennan made his mark as a scholar with a "realist"
critique of international law, finding the "legalistic-moralistic approach
to international problems" to be "the most serious fault" in American
foreign policy.[13] By January of 1982, however, he confessed to a whole-
sale change in his thinking in this regard, and was even ready to adopt
the radical world federalist reforms advocated by Grenville Clark and
Louis Sohn in their 1958 book on "World Peace Through World Law":

> To many of us—and I think particularly those of us who had been
> in the practice of diplomacy—these ideas looked, at the time,

impractical, if not naïve. Today, two decades later, and in the light of what has occurred in the interval, the logic of them is more compelling.[14]

While it was "still too early for their realization on a universal basis," when humanity finally does "begin to come seriously to grips" with creating a more governed world, "it is to the carefully thought-out and profoundly humane ideas of Grenville Clark and Louis Sohn that they will have to turn for inspiration and guidance."[15]

Finally, one of the most hopeful prospects for future changes in attitudes falls under the heading of increasing understanding amongst peoples. If one looks historically at relations between countries, there is considerable basis for hope. For centuries, the English and the French, for example, spilled millions of gallons of each others' blood on battlefields all over the world. And now, of course, they are firm allies. One can also point to our own recent relations with Germany and Japan, once bitter enemies, now firm allies. Evolution occurs in the social sphere as well as in the biological sphere. And increasingly these changes in attitudes are capable of taking place over shorter periods of time.

Thus, taking an inventory of our current stock of potential "enemies"—Russia, China, and portions of the Muslim World—we can ask ourselves how might our relations with them improve over time. And what might the United States do to improve these relations?

For one thing, we could start by treating other countries with respect. This is a minimum. We need to resist the temptation to call other nations names, such as the "Evil Empire"[16] or the "Axil of Evil in the World." This does nothing to advance our national security interests. Secondly, it is unwise to unnecessarily threaten them, since fear is a dangerous emotion to arouse in any potential enemy. Which raises an important point. What is the one thing that the United States could do right now to decrease fear and therefore encourage liberalizing elements in Russia, China, and the Muslim world? Getting rid of all nuclear weapons. As we have argued above, these weapons themselves generate incredible fear which distorts our relations with other countries. Just as there are unintended negative consequences of war, so too there may be unintended positive consequences of the abolition of nuclear weapons.

Although it will seem naïve to make such predictions in the current climate, if one takes the long view it is not unrealistic to expect the gradual liberalization of Russia, China, and even the Muslim world in the next decade or so.

Russia. Looking briefly at Russia: despite the tremendous hurdles democracy has had to face and will no doubt continue to face, the seeds of democracy have nevertheless been planted by the likes of Andrei Sakharov and Mikhail Gorbachev and Alexei Navalny and countless heroic others, and will eventually bear fruit.[17] Mainstream thinkers already predict that Russia will one day join NATO and the European Union.[18]

China. We simply must have good relations with China, and cannot allow them to become the next "designated enemy" for the United States. Aside from the obvious trade and international financial reasons, China can increase its nuclear weapons several-fold at any time, having obviously not done so until now due to a conscious decision to maintain only a minimal deterrence force. Despite the differences in our social and political systems, and despite increasing sources of conflict,[19] we must never allow these differences and disputes to get out of hand, relying instead upon international dispute resolution to resolve these problems.

Islam. We are currently experiencing dramatic post-9/11 fear[20] and outright Islamaphobia.[21] But this will not last. While the dialogic process and events in the real world are likely to get rather ugly in the short run,[22] in the long run, we will eventually come to our senses and come to appreciate once again the value of the ideals of tolerance and religious freedom. Religious and gender rights reform is already under way in most of the Muslim world,[23] and the vast majority of Muslim countries favor democracy over theocracy.[24] Nor need we fear what some have called a "clash of civilizations."[25] Rather, we have every right, given long-term trends, to expect the continued realization of the universal values in the UN Charter and the Universal Declaration of Human Rights.[26]

It could be objected that all I have demonstrated above is that peace (in the form of increased understanding) leads to peace, by definition. And indeed there is some truth in ICJ Judge Stephen Schwebel's comment that "arbitration is not the way to prevent war; it is rather a product of peace."[27] Nevertheless, while some degree of consensus and good will is a necessary prelude to arbitration, the availability of arbitration on a regular basis and the development over time of an international norm making arbitration and other forms of international dispute resolution mandatory would (a) allow nations to back off gracefully from otherwise war-precipitating confrontations, and (b) reinforce the rule-of-law-abiding and international-norm-respecting behavior of nations. In other words, good will alone is insufficient; institutional arrangements are also necessary.[28]

Major upcoming social changes

The second category of indicators that a new day is coming for the global rule of law is that we are on the verge of major social changes in all the classic United Nations categories: human rights, economic and environmental regulation, economic development, and peace.

Taking human rights seriously

In the past 60 years there has been "a veritable revolution in transforming visions of international human rights into reality."[29] Many experts in the 1970s were predicting that apartheid would never end, but in 1994 South Africa's white parliament voted itself out of existence, ending 342 years of white rule.[30] America recently elected (twice) its first black president.

Consider next gender rights. My alma mater, Harvard Law School, did not admit women until 1950! There was no right to even vote until 1921.[31] And the venerable U.S. Supreme Court Justice Joseph P. Bradley wrote this in an 1873 decision upholding the exclusion of women from law practice:

> [T]he civil law, as well as nature herself, has always recognized a wide difference in the respective spheres and destinies of man and woman … The paramount destiny and mission of woman [sic] are to fulfill the noble and benign offices of wife and mother. This is the law of the Creator [sick].[32]

Nowadays, of course, there is nothing unusual about female U.S. Supreme Court Justices. Given the key role that woman can and will play in eventually securing a lasting peace, this fairly recent history in our own country augurs well for the future.[33]

Economic and environmental regulation

Appears to be "the next big thing" on the international horizon if the sheer need for it is any indication. Since this is not a book on that topic, all that will be done here is to hint at some of the likely upcoming changes in areas such as international financial regulation, regulation of tax havens, minimal worker safety, and social benefits legislation, as well as global environmental governance.[34] A major source of the problem is the "race to the bottom phenomenon," whereby wealthy multi-national corporations and others are able to use the forces of the global market to force countries to abandon or eviscerate social welfare standards in order to attract investment and save jobs. As stated rather succinctly by David Kennedy:

> Speaking loosely, and to put it in the starkest terms, with economic globalization and the continued loss of public capacity, large swaths of the world will, in twenty years, have whatever social security system, whatever environmental regime, whatever labor law, whatever wage rate, prevails in China.[35]

In short, something more substantial than the occasional chat amongst the G-20 is necessary. There is a need for a global economic regulation establishing minimum standards to prevent the race-to-the-bottom phenomenon.

Development

There is finally a new research agenda afoot to test what actually works and what doesn't work in the area of economic development, and we will soon have the benefits of that research.[36]

Peace

Although some short-term steps toward abolition of nuclear weapons have long been identified, such as de-alerting nuclear missiles, a Comprehensive Test Ban Treaty, and a Fissile Materials Cut-Off Treaty,[37] there is a serious movement afoot to begin work on an abolition convention.[38] Further, instead of STRATCOM's vision of Full Spectrum Dominance in space and under the seas,[39] which is as unrealistic as our earlier expectation of maintaining a permanent lead in the nuclear arms race,[40] we will need to adopt a cooperative approach focused on securing global security.[41] In addition, as previously noted, there are two short-term goals which would be both easy to effectuate and of huge immediate advantage: (1) a non-use treaty re nuclear weapons, and (2) compulsory mediation, which would solve the vast majority of conflicts while imposing no real infringement upon national sovereignty.

A whole new world

We are living in one of the most extraordinary periods of change in the evolution of this planet. We live in a post-Hiroshima, post-Sputnik, post-Moon landing, post-civil rights, post-Cold War, post-Genome

Project, post-TV and internet world.[42] We live in a world where a Russian plutocrat, Mikhail Prokhorov, just bought the New Jersey Nets. In 1990, Dwight D. Eisenhower's granddaughter, Susan Eisenhower, married the former head of the Soviet space program.[43] Walt Disney is over in China, with a sophisticated language-learning program (with interactive video monitors, virtual animals, local and Western instructors, 300 songs, 60 books, and a price tag per child of $1800, with waiting lists in several cities), teaching English to Chinese children as young as two.[44] It was not even front-page news when a joint Russian-American space crew safely touched down on September 25, 2010, in their Russian-built Soyuz space capsule in the central steppes of Kazakhstan after six months aboard the International Space Station.[45] The number of autocracies is steadily declining.[46] In sum, in the very midst of what we inevitably view as insurmountable problems, we appear to be approaching the Grotian moment when humanity finally replaces the use of force with the global rule of law.[47]

Synergistic nature of social change

Of course, all the above changes in attitudes and major social progress will inevitably play together. Progress on one front will facilitate progress on other fronts. Thus, progress on economic development and human rights will facilitate the kinds of changes in attitudes needed for significant arms reductions and a greater willingness to rely on global legal structures. Arms reductions, in turn, will allow greater economic and human development and a resultant blossoming of humanity's creative capacity for good. Deeper arms reductions will no doubt depend upon progress in building alternative security systems and stronger international legal institutions. And even though there will be the usual setbacks along the way, the historic trend is clear. We are gradually working our way to a better world, one that accepts the universal values of the UN Charter and the necessity for adopting alternatives to war, an international dispute resolution system.[48]

The USA as both the problem and the solution

But if "a new world is possible," then, as the new WILPF (Women's International League for Peace and Freedom) slogan has it, "a new United States is necessary."[49] Historically, it was the United States that led the way in generous and far-sighted global initiatives. But lately America has faltered and taken a fear-driven turn inward, toward what one former government official candidly called "the dark side," and it has done us no good, and much harm. For world opinion matters. World opinion about certain of our actions taken in the past has directly influenced terrorists to undertake the horrific crimes they have committed. Thus, whether we are smart enough to realize it or not, our future safety and security—that of our children—depends on world opinion.

And so, what we probably most need to do, as George Kennan recommended in 1957, is to address "our own American failings, ... the things that we are ashamed of in our own eyes, or that worry us."[50] This is, of course, a rather sizeable task, and we cannot hope to tackle the full "list" here. But one of the most dramatic failures in American history has been our failure to heed the remarkable message of President Dwight David Eisenhower in his Farewell Address of January 17, 1961. In it, the former five-star general and Supreme Allied Commander said:

> This conjunction of an immense military establishment and a large arms industry is new in the American experience. The total influence—economic, political, even spiritual—is felt in every city, every statehouse, every office of the federal government. We recognize the imperative need for this development. Yet we must not fail to comprehend its grave implications. Our toil, resources and livelihood are all involved; so is the very structure of our society.
>
> In the councils of government, we must guard against the acquisition of unwarranted influence, whether sought or unsought, by the military-industrial complex. The potential for disastrous rise of misplaced power exists and will persist.[51]

Eisenhower was, of course, all too prophetic. Not only was there a great "potential" for the disastrous rise of misplaced power, that potential has been massively and frighteningly realized in the five decades since Eisenhower's speech.[52] We now have, it is safe to say, what amounts to a military-industrial-congressional-academic-think-tank legalized-theft complex, whereby leading defense contractors make sizeable contributions to congressmen and, in return, those congressmen fight for appropriations that result in huge contracts for said contractors, contracts that are often a thousand times or more the size of said contributions,[53] which is not good. It has gotten so bad that ordinary people have lost all faith in our congress, whether such cynicism is totally justified or not.[54]

What can be done? One thing minimally necessary is to require at least disclosure of those making large campaign contributions so that we can identify who is currying influence, whether "sought or unsought."[55] Secondly, to regain control of our democracy, we need campaign finance reform, even if a constitutional amendment is required.[56]

Finally, and most importantly, our major focus must be on finding the levers of social change that will move us from a fear-driven culture of war to a culture of peace. In order for that to take place, it will take one thing: education.[57] In the end, there will be no substitute for the hard work of educating ourselves and others. In order for our society to escape the fatal mindset into which we have fallen, whereby war seems to be the answer to every problem[58] and international law and international institutions are openly sneered at, we must educate ourselves to what Albert Einstein and Bertrand Russell called "a new way of thinking," to an understanding that in the nuclear age nations must find "peaceful means for the settlement of all matters of dispute between them."[59] Specifically, the concepts of alternative dispute resolution that have become so prevalent in our domestic legal context need to be extended to international dispute resolution, something that has been totally neglected in recent decades, even amongst our current elites (including the president, secretary of state, secretary of defense, and almost all academics).

Rethinking an old theory

Since 1789, the idea of peaceful settlement of international conflict via the world rule of law has had some prominent proponents. Jeremy Bentham had a quite comprehensive (and surprisingly modern) vision of the overall concept (as did Hans Kelsen and John J. McCloy). It was perhaps the arbitration aspect of "world peace through law" that was a key attraction for Presidents Grant and Taft. The growth of the global rule of law seemed to be of special interest to Arthur Larson and Charles Rhyne. And a credible UN Peace Force was a high priority for President Theodore Roosevelt. It is hard to know what part or parts of WPTL will be taken up in the future, and in what sequence. There are, as Jane Addams observes, "such unexpected turnings in the paths of moral evolution."[60] But all the basic components seem to finally be in place for this next big step upward in human progress. Moreover, there appears to be an amazing dovetailing of purposes behind the above components whereby: (1) nuclear weapons have made abolition necessary; (2) abolition will result in the trust needed for nations to rely on global dispute resolution; and (3) the existence of global dispute resolution mechanisms will allow nations to abandon nuclear weapons with confidence.

What we propose is neither all that new nor all that radical. The central crux of our twenty-first century version of WPTL—compulsory international dispute resolution—is an idea that is at once so intuitively obvious as to be almost embarrassing, while at the same time encompassing a complex mosaic of social justice initiatives. The core of the proposal, however, as envisioned by Jeremy Bentham and others, is a three-legged stool, with each leg of major importance: (1) reductions in offensive weaponry, in particular the complete abolition of nuclear weapons; (2) an international court with compulsory jurisdiction, preceded by compulsory negotiation, mediation, and arbitration; and (3) effective enforcement mechanisms, ranging from the force of world opinion to various other non-military sanctions to an international peace force.

This plan is basically what was proposed but not accepted at the Hague Peace Conferences of 1899 and 1907. To be specific, due to the opposition of Germany, the Hague Conventions ended up rejecting (1) arms reductions; (2) compulsory arbitration; and (3) any realistic enforcement mechanisms. In short, the views of the visionaries were rejected, and the views of the "realists" of the era prevailed. But in this the nuclear age, WPTL is now the only practical alternative. While each of the WPTL components is individually very worthwhile, by combining a Nuclear Weapons Abolition Convention with a Global Rule of Law Treaty, we would finally have a comprehensive system of "world peace through law."[61]

Moreover, even if we do not immediately effectuate the entirety of this tripartite plan, partial steps along the way would be of immense help. For instance, if we secure near-abolition of nuclear weapons along with at least a freeze of conventional weaponry, accompanied by the key component of compulsory mediation by the major powers, this would all by itself constitute an enormous improvement in global security.

A world without war

We need to begin to imagine a world without war, something ironically made possible by the very existential threat we now face. For if nuclear war is, as is oft-times stated, "unimaginable," then we need to make a world without war imaginable. It took us two-million years to evolve from our last common ancestor with chimps. How much might we develop in the next two-million years—provided we give ourselves that long? In the meantime, given the rapid pace of cultural evolution, it is in our power in just the next decade to secure a whole new lease on life.

It is rather difficult to be overly optimistic at this precise moment when America's performance on the world stage has been so abysmal. Yet this selfsame disastrous era in American "diplomacy" ought to have proven to any reasonable person the hazards of global illegalism and the severe costs of being the world's policeman. Thus, the silver lining to our recent mistakes is that they have paved the way for America to return to the role it once played in the world.

If we continue as we have in the recent past, pursuing what we perceive to be our narrow national interest without regard to what others think, then we will eventually decline and fall, like all other domineering "empires" in the past. But if we adopt a new paradigm of international cooperation and the global rule of law, we will transform the world. In putting it this way, we are of course opening ourselves to the accusation of being called "idealistic." Well, of course, it's idealistic; it better be. For without idealism precisely none of the major social changes in history would have taken place. WPTL is worth every bit of our idealist energies, for preventing nuclear war is "not only the great issue of our times but the greatest issue of all time."[62]

We stand amidst a stunning universe that is 93-billion light years[63] in diameter, poised to continue a development—human life—that is nothing short of a miracle.[64] It is not just us, of course. It is the entire megaverse, including our Earth, spinning through space at 66,000 miles per hour around the Sun, which holds us in place from 93-million miles away by the magic of gravity[65] while supplying us with the heat and light and energy necessary for life; the Daddy Long Legs, with its tiny eyes and brain somehow able to function; and all of "nature as [we have] known and trusted [it]."[66] Thomas Berry offers an intriguing thought:

> If the dynamics of the universe from the beginning shaped the course of the heavens, lighted the sun, and formed the Earth, if this same dynamism brought forth the continents and seas and atmosphere, if it awakened life in the primordial cell and then brought into being the unnumbered variety of living beings, and finally brought us into being and guided us safely through the turbulent centuries, there is reason to believe that this same guiding process is precisely what has awakened us in our present understanding of ourselves and our relation to this stupendous process. Sensitized to such guidance from the very structure and functioning of the universe, we can have confidence in the future that awaits the human venture.[67]

What is our future? Will we have the fortitude and intelligence, after thousands of years of war, to finally secure a lasting peace? Despite the many complexities surrounding the matter, in the end, if we can do one thing—turn to global alternative dispute resolution mechanisms to resolve international conflict—we will have solved the problem of peace, surely the most important endeavor of the human race.

Notes

1 Many years ago, he approached me at a peace conference, and said, "young man, please take this book." It was A Common Sense Guide to World Peace (1985). Cf. Nadia Khomani, "'It was as if I had peered into hell': the man who brought the Nazi death squads to justice," *The Guardian*, February 7, 2017 (brief bio of Ferencz) and Lesley Stahl, "60 Minutes: What the last Nuremberg prosecutor alive wants the world to know," May 7, 2017, www.cbsnew.com.
2 Benjamin B. Ferencz, "A World of Peace under the Rule of Law: The View from America," 6 *Wash. U. Global Studies L. Rev.* 664, 672 (2007) (emphasis added).
3 Oliver Wendell Holmes Quotations.
4 See Kristin E. Holmes, "Music as a peace-building initiative," *Philadelphia Inquirer*, March 7, 2013, p. B-1 (Palestinian-Israeli youth music ensemble); David Patrick Stearns, "Critic's Notebook: The fierce music of Estonia [and] Latvia," *Philadelphia Inquirer*, August 22, 2010, p. H-1 (Latvian and Estonian composers were part of a Baltic "singing revolution" which led to the demise of Soviet domination of their countries); and "Iran's Islamic Revolution," *Bloomberg Businessweek*, May 29–June 4, 2017, at 15 ("if music becomes more popular, no one will listen to the imams.").
5 Many years ago I attended a peace gathering up in the mountains of Montana at an abandoned resort. At night we gathered around a large fire. Seated next to me was a pony-tailed young man who said that his group believed in what they called "total tactics," meaning this "pushing multiple fronts at once" approach.
6 See generally "World at War," Special Issue, *The Defense Monitor*, vol. 36 no. 1 (January/February 2007); Joshua S. Goldstein, Winning the War on War: The Decline of Conflict Worldwide (2011); Steven Pinker, The Better Angels of Our Nature: Why Violence Has Declined (2011); and Joseph Cirincione, Bomb Scare: The History & Future of Nuclear Weapons, at 155–156 (2007). But see David Swanson, War No More: The Case for Abolition, at 131–140 (2013).
7 See, e.g., Bruce M. Russett, "Preventing Violent Conflict through the Kantian Peace," Chapter 12, in Peter Wallensteen, ed., Preventing Violent Conflicts: Past Record and Future Challenges (1998) (democracies rarely fight each other).
8 See, e.g., Michael W. Doyle, Ways of War and Peace: Realism, Liberalism, and Socialism, Chapter 7 (1997).
9 Cf. Charles J. Moxley, Jr., John Burroughs, & Jonathan Granoff, "Nuclear Weapons and Compliance with International Humanitarian Law and the Nuclear Non-Proliferation Treaty, 34 *Fordham Int'l L.J.* 595 (2011).
10 Robert S. McNamara, "Apocalypse Soon," Foreign Policy (May/June 2005), at 29 (agreeing with William Perry's estimate of over 50% likelihood of nuclear detonation on U.S. targets within a decade).

11 See Charles S. Rhyne, International Law: The Substance, Processes, Procedures and Institutions for World Peace with Justice, at 608 (1971): "Public opinion fluctuates until it crystallizes, but when it crystallizes it becomes an almost uncontrollable factor in the affairs of humankind. More and more, a vast worldwide desire is growing into a demand that law replace force as the controlling factor in the fate of humanity." Cf. also Abraham Lincoln ("Public sentiment is everything. With public sentiment, nothing can fail; without public sentiment, nothing can succeed. Hence, he who molds public sentiment goes farther than he who drafts statutes or pronounces decisions. He is making statutes or decisions possible or impossible to be executed." Emphasis added.) and Victor Hugo ("All the forces in the world are not so powerful as an idea whose time has come.").

12 See Fred Inglis, The Cruel Peace: Everyday Life and the Cold War, at 89 (1991) ("He was the most important shaper of the most important foreign policy decisions that his country, superpower of the world, would take for fifty years.").

13 George Kennan, American Diplomacy 1900–1950, at 82 (1951).

14 George Kennan, "On Nuclear War," *New York Review of Books*, at 11 (January 21, 1982).

15 Id. George Kennan was also an early proponent of nuclear weapons abolition. See, e.g., George F. Kennan, Russia, The Atom and the West, at 55 (1957) (even towards the beginning of his conversion, he called nuclear weapons "suicidal" and "sterile and hopeless") and George F. Kennan, The Nuclear Delusion: Soviet-American Relations in the Atomic Age, at 204–207 (1976).

16 I have a "Many Paths to Peace" slideshow, and one of the slides is a charming cartoon showing Reagan and Gromyko, with Reagan saying: "Well, Andrei, be sure to give my regard to Comrade Vader and the whole gang back at the Empire." Of course, Reagan himself famously took back the above-quoted words.

17 See, e.g., Trudy Rubin, "A Cause for Optimism: Russia's Young People," *Philadelphia Inquirer*, March 8, 2012, at A2 (utilizing her classic "ear-to-the-ground" technique, she concludes that "political change here is inevitable") and "The Birth of Russian Citizenry," *Economist*, December 17, 2001, at 92. But cf. "Russia v America," *Economist*, October 8, 2016, at 46 (recent adverse developments).

18 See Trudy Rubin, "How Russia could become U.S. ally," *Philadelphia Inquirer*, June 21, 2015, at C-1. See also Stephen J. Cimbala, Nuclear Weapons and Cooperative Security in the 21st Century: The New Disorder, at 24–25 (2010) ("... NATO could offer Russia a full membership on the understanding that it would have to meet the alliance's requirements for political democracy and military transparency.") and William J. Perry, My Journey at the Nuclear Brink, Chapter 16 (2015) (in the mid-90s, Russia attended many NATO meetings, and contributed Russian brigade to NATO peacekeeping forces in Bosnia).

19 See Chapter 11 supra at note 15 (South China Sea disputes). See generally, David Shambough, China's Future, at 144–155 (2016). Cf. also John Pomfret, The Beautiful Country and the Middle Kingdom: America and China, 1776 to the Present (2016) (an excellent history of the love-hate relationship).

20 See Benjamin B. Ferencz, "A World of Peace," supra, at 671 ("I've never seen the people of this country so frightened."). Cf. generally, Hugh Gusterson & Catherine Besteman, eds., The Insecure American, How We Got Here & What We Should Do About It (2010).
21 See, e.g., Chris McGreal, "The US blogger on a mission to halt 'Islamic takeover,'" *The Guardian*, August 20, 2010, p. 20 (Pam Geller heads group called "Stop the Islamization of America," claiming Muslims want to impose sharia law in America; Islam-bashing increasing post-9/11, with politicians using the issue as a wedge); Tony Norman, "America's Dark Age of Islamophobia," *Philadelphia Inquirer*, December 16, 2011, p. A-27 (decrying American ignorance of Islamic contributions to Western civilization, e.g., algebra, trigonometry, optics, astronomy, the classics, and Arabic numbers); and Arun Kundnani, The Muslims Are Coming! Islamophobia, Extremism, and the Domestic War on Terror (2014).
22 Exposing, e.g., some of the genocidal and otherwise untoward statements in the canonical works of each of the Abrahamic religions. See Karen Armstrong, The Battle for God: Fundamentalism in Judaism, Christianity, and Islam (2000).
23 See, e.g., Pankaj Mushra, "The Misunderstood Muslims," *New York Review of Books*, November 17, 2005, at 15–16; Rabbi Marc Schneier & Imam Shamsi Ali, Sons of Abraham: A Candid Conversation about the Issues that Divide and Unite Jews and Muslims (2014); and www.strategic foresight.com (working for an inclusive world).
24 See Charles Kenny, "The Convergence of Civilizations," *Foreign Policy* (January/February 2013), at 22 (98% of Egyptians and 92% of Iranians favor democracy).
25 See Anne Norton, On the Muslim Question, Chapter 10 (2013) ("There is No Clash of Civilizations") (contrary to Samuel Huntingdon thesis, universal Islamic values are broadly compatible with liberalism) and Tamara Sonn, Is Islam an Enemy of the West?, at 7, 106–113 (2016) (attacking Huntingdon's "shoddy scholarship" and erroneous views of Islam; contrary to popular perception, "Muslim religious authorities … unanimously condemn terrorism").
26 See Bessma Momani, Arab Dawn: Arab Youth and the Demographic Dividend They Will Bring (2015) (Internet opening up Islam, allowing younger generation to distance themselves from older traditional practices; increasing intermarriage outside tribal and ethnic lines; increasing cosmopolitanism; increasing support for women working and other gender rights; huge increase in study abroad and resultant "social remittances"; strong belief in free market and entrepreneurship). But cf. Sam Harris & Maajid Nawaz, Islam and the Future of Tolerance: A Dialogue (2015) (the process of Islamic liberalization will be difficult).
27 S.M. Schwebel, "Comments on Professor Pinto," in A.H.A. Soons, ed., International Arbitration, supra, at 108 (1990).
28 See Roger Fisher, Points of Choice: International Crises and the Role of Law, at 31–32 (1978) (need a pre-existing institution with jurisdiction to resolve disputes) and J. Kirk Boyd, 2048: Humanity's Agreement to Live Together: The International Movement for Enforceable Human Rights (2010).
29 Paul Gordon Lauren, The Evolution of International Human Rights: Visions Seen, at 265 (3rd ed. 2011). Accord, Paul Kennedy, The Parliament

of Man: The Past, Present, and Future of the United Nations, Chapter 6 (2006).

30 See Kennedy, supra, at 201–202. See also Nelson Mandela, Long Walk to Freedom: The Autobiography of Nelson Mandela (1994).

31 See Jamie Stiehm, "Celebrating 90 years of suffrage," *Philadelphia Inquirer*, August 29, 2010, p. C-1 col. 1 (excellent synopsis of women's suffrage movement, ca. 1848–1920).

32 *Bradwell v. Illinois*, 83 U.S. 130, 141 (1873) (concurring, joined by two other justices).

33 See Valerie M. Hudson, Bonnie Ballif-Spanvill, Mary Caprioli, & Chad F. Emmett, Sex and World Peace (2012) and Judith L. Hand, "To Abolish War," 2 *J. of Aggression, Conflict & Peace Research* 44–56 (2010) (need Egalitarian Revolution to end war).

34 See, e.g., Michael J. Casey, The Unfair Trade: How Our Broken Financial System Destroys the Middle Class (2012) (senior economics editor of Wall Street Journal argues for need for greater global financial regulation); Ronen Palan, Richard Murphy, & Christian Chavagneux, Tax Havens: How Globalization Really Works (2010) (approximately 56 major tax/regulatory/secrecy havens involving 2-million companies and $12 trillion in assets, result in annual tax loss estimated at $255 billion; GAO report shows that by now 60% of large U.S. corporations pay no taxes; havens also hide risky debt instruments, facilitate corruption, and cause the deaths of over 250,000 children per year due to illegal capital flight and lost tax revenue); James Gustave Speth & Peter M. Haas, Global Environmental Governance (2006); and Pierre De Senarclens and Ali Kazancigil, Regulating Globalization: Critical Approaches to Global Governance (2007).

35 David Kennedy, "The Mystery of Global Governance," in Jeffrey L. Dunoff & Joel P. Trachtman, eds., Ruling the World? Constitutionalism, International Law, and Global Governance, at 59 (2009). See also Eyal Benvenisti, "Exit and Voice in the Age of Globalization," 98 Mich. L. Rev. 167, 201 (1999) ("The race to the bottom precludes collective action measures that would promote better labor standards, protect consumers and the environment, and allocate shared resources in an optimal and sustained way. Local and multinational firms exploit these failures and externalize a substantial part of their costs on both their fellow citizens and foreign communities."); William Greider, Who Will Tell the People: The Betrayal of American Democracy, at 378 (1992) ("The global competition for cost advantage effectively weakens the sovereignty of every nation by promoting a fierce contest among countries for lower public standards ... This reality constitutes the largest challenge confronting American democracy ... ."); and David Rothkopf, Power, Inc: The Epic Rivalry between Big Business and Government—and the Reckoning That Lies Ahead (2012).

36 See, e.g., Wikipedia re Professor Esther Duflo, French economist, co-founder of MIT's Poverty Action Lab. See also Ha-Joon Chang, 23 Things They Don't Tell You about Capitalism, Chapters 7, 11, 15 (2010).

37 For an excellent collection of short-term ideas, see Ploughshares Fund, "10 Big Nuclear Ideas for the Next President" (November 2016). Cf. also Greg Thielmann, "Can the INF Treaty Survive? Putin's New Missile Presents A Major Test for Arms Control," *Arms Control Today*, at 6,

13 (April 2017) (possible to "leapfrog current compliance disputes" with broader approach).

38 See Sharon Squassoni, "A controversial ban and the long game to delegitimize nuclear weapons," *Bulletin of the Atomic Scientists*, July 10, 2017 (122 nations adopt Treaty on the Prohibition of Nuclear Weapons, but none of nuclear weapons states join it).

39 See Patrick Tucker, "Will Subdrones Cause World War III?," www. defenseone.com/technology/2015/09/will-subdrones-cause-world-war-iii/120383?oref=defenseone_today_nl (September 7, 2015) (projected use of unmanned underwater vehicles in contested waters of Pacific, Persian Gulf, and Arctic).

40 See, e.g., Bill Gertz, "Russia Building Nuclear-Armed Drone Submarine," *National Security* (September 8, 2015).

41 See Mike Moore, Twilight War: The Folly of U.S. Space Dominance (2008) (compelling arguments against the weaponization of space, and for extending the Outer Space Treaty of 1967 to non-nuclear weapons).

42 If Matt Ridley's "collective brain" concept is valid, think of the size of our modern worldwide interconnected brain. Matt Ridley, The Rational Optimist: How Prosperity Evolves, at 82 (2010). See also Science Channel, "When Does Life Begin?" (2013) (Francis Heylighen: global brain is becoming exponentially more intelligent).

43 See Susan Eisenhower, Breaking Free: A Memoir of Love and Revolution (1995) (an amazing story). Cf. id. at 101: "A wave of rebellion washed over me. *This goddam Cold War could destroy this gentle wonderful man—and maybe even me. And for what? So, our governments can score points about the righteousness of our respective systems—and tell our people that massive overkill capacity is necessary to secure the peace? It seemed so ironic that love could be shattered in the name of peace.*"

44 *The Economist*, August 28, 2010, at 52 ("Middle Kingdom meets Magic Kingdom").

45 "Space crew lands in Kazakhstan," *Philadelphia Inquirer*, September 26, 2010, p. A5. Cf. also "Three astronauts back from station," *Philadelphia Inquirer*, April 28, 2012, p. A6 (two Russians and an American, who nobody in America could name, returned to Earth in Russian space capsule; their names: Anton Shkaplerov, Anatoly Ivanishin, and Daniel Burbank).

46 When one commentator back in 1965 toted up the number of countries that might be threatened by limitations on the number of internal police forces, he was able to name quite a few countries. See Louis Lusky, "Four Problems in Lawmaking for Peace," 80 Pol. Sc. Q. 341, 354–355 (1965) (citing as examples China, USSR, Spain, Portugal, Hungary, Yugoslavia, Indonesia, and South Africa). And now democratic revolutions have occurred in almost all of those countries. Also cf. John Timpane, *Philadelphia Inquirer*, January 27, 2011, p. A-1, "Turmoil in the streets—and on the Web" ("When dictator Zine el-Abidine Ben Ali fled Tunisia on January 14, it was the first time in history that Twitter, Facebook, and other social media had helped bring down a government.").

47 See Mark W. Janis, An Introduction to International Law, at 176 (4th ed. 2003) ("It may be that we have now reached a pass comparable to that when Grotius wrote. Perhaps the horrors of war are again so vivid that there will be incentive enough to fashion new legal limits to control the

use of force by states."); Richard Falk, "The First Normative Global Revolution?: The Uncertain Political Future of Globalization," in Mehdi Mazaffari, ed., Globalizations and Civilizations, at 51–76 (2002) (arguing that a series of recent developments have set the stage for a new surge of global norms); and Joshua S. Goldstein, "World Peace Could Be Closer Than You Think," Foreign Policy, 53 (September/October 2011).

48 Of course, as already noted, it will take a "total systems" approach. Just as the military-industrial complex supports and sustains a militaristic approach to world peace, so too, an alternative-dispute-resolution law-based approach will need systemic support from a vast array of sources.

49 As with many aphorisms, this one is probably not entirely true. For if America fails to lead, others may take the initiative. See, e.g., middlepowersinitiative.org. And no one country, however important, can solve the problem of peace. More generally, the basic WPTL concept is not just an American idea; it is equally, as we have seen, an ancient Greek idea, as well as a Czech (King George of Bohemia), British (Jeremy Bentham), French (Leon Bourgeois), and Russian (Mikhail Gorbachev) idea. In short, it is a universal idea, reflecting a growing recognition of the universal human right to peace. See Douglas Roche [Canadian], The Human Right to Peace (2003).

50 George F. Kennan, Russia, the Atom and the West, at 13 (1957) (emphasis added) and Richard N. Haass, Foreign Policy Begins at Home: The Case for Putting America's House in Order (2013).

51 Also in the speech is this little-noticed sentence: "[W]e must also be alert to the ... danger that public policy could itself become the captive of a scientific-technological elite." One thing that will be required during the abolition of nuclear weapons is the redirection of the activities of the nuclear labs toward peaceful programs. See Judith Reppy, "U.S. nuclear laboratories in a nuclear-zero world," *Bulletin of the Atomic Scientists*, vol. 66 no. 4, at 42 (July/August 2010).

52 Cf. generally, the documentary "Why We Fight," by Eugene Jarecki (2005). Cf. also Rebecca U. Thorpe, The American Warfare State: The Domestic Politics of Military Spending (2014) (detailed empirical studies reveal systematic congressional bias in favor of military spending in excess of security needs and in favor of interventionism, especially in districts heavily dependent on defense subcontracts, and also due to increased use of volunteer army, private security firms, and deficit spending).

53 See, e.g., William Hartung, How Much Are You Making in the War Daddy? A Quick and Dirty Guide to War Profiteering in the Bush Administration, at 120, 132 (2003) (top three defense contractors gave contributions of $4.7 million in 2002, receiving $41 billion in contracts in the same year).

54 See, e.g., Lawrence Lessig, Republic, Lost: How Money Corrupts Congress—And a Plan to Stop It, at 167 (2011) ("80 percent of Americans surveyed ... believed government was controlled by 'a few big interests looking out for themselves.'"). But cf. Joseph N. DiStefano, "Senator: Congress is less corrupt than ever," *Philadelphia Inquirer*, September 5, 2010, p. C3 (Sen. Ted Kaufman).

55 As would be required by S. 3628, the DISCLOSE ("Democracy is Strengthened by Casting Light on Spending in Elections") Act.

56 See Richard L. Hasen, Plutocrats United: Campaign Money, the Supreme Court, and the Distortion of American Elections (2016) (argues that a

constitutional amendment is *not* necessary and that "political equality is a compelling interest that ... justifies both 'leveling up' through campaign vouchers and 'leveling down' through generous individual campaign spending limits").

The crux of the U.S. Supreme Court's holding in *Citizens United*, which seems to have escaped the attention of most commentators, is the following language: "[W]e now conclude that independent expenditures, including those made by corporations, do not give rise to corruption or the appearance of corruption ... The appearance of influence ... will not cause the electorate to lose faith in democracy." *Citizens United v. FEC*, 558 U.S. 310, 352, 354 (2010) (emphasis added). Both statements are, of course, demonstrably false.

57 A long-ago collaborator, Bill Wickersham, sent me a draft of a speech (undated, ca. 1984) which has these keywords: "When people tell me there is nothing they can do to prevent nuclear war, my usual reply is, 'Yes there is something you can do. You can educate yourself and others. Education is an essential ingredient for the solution of any social problem.' In order for us to free ourselves of the nuclear warfare trap, we obviously have to have social and political change. Social and political change requires attitudinal change. Attitudinal change requires education. Education requires time, money and energy."

58 See Rosa Brooks, How Everything Became War and the Military Became Everything: Tales from the Pentagon (2016) and Andrew J. Bacevich, Washington Rules: America's Path to Permanent War (2010). See also Paul Fussell, Thank God for the Atom Bomb, at 115–116 (1988) (Admiral Gene LaRoque [Ret.]: "Our military runs our foreign policy. The State Department simply goes around and tidies up the messes the military makes."); Andrew J. Bacevich, America's War for the Greater Middle East, at 362 (2016) ("Time and again ... U.S. military power, unleashed rather than held in abeyance, has met outright failure, produced results other than those intended, or proved to be largely irrelevant."); and Dominic Tierney, The Right Way to Lose a War: America in an Age of Unwinnable Conflicts, at 18 (2015) (awesome military capabilities are "a constant temptation to use force.").

59 The "Russell-Einstein Manifesto" (July 9, 1955), www.pugwash.org.

60 Jane Addams, Peace and Bread in Time of War, at 83 (1922). Accord, Luuk Van Middelaar, The Passage to Europe: How a Continent Became a Union, at xii (2013) ("No project, no treaty can anticipate the creativity of history ... .").

61 The two projects may well prove to be necessary adjuncts of one another: i.e., just as abolition may provide both the practical necessity and the moral impetus to secure WPTL, so too WPTL may be the missing link to securing abolition. Cf. Perkovich and Acton, supra, Abolishing Nuclear Weapons: A Debate, at 106 (countries "would need to be brought into processes to determine how to manage international enforcement of rules and peaceful relationships well before later steps to eliminate nuclear arsenals could be taken.") and Securing Our Survival, supra, at 175: "As Trevor Findlay (2006) points out, 'complete nuclear disarmament implies not just a significant evolution in verification, but an evolution in the international system. States will have to change their attitudes towards the limits of sovereignty, the rule of international law and governance of

the international system, particularly in regard to enforcement, if nuclear disarmament is ever to be negotiated."

While Perkovich and Acton opine that "[t]he eight nuclear-armed states will not be able to collectively envisage a prohibition of nuclear weapons until conflicts cent[e]ring on Taiwan, Kashmir, Palestine, and (perhaps) the Russian periphery are resolved, or at least durably stabilized," id. at 152, they fail to consider that shy of actual resolution of conflicts; there is another possibility: a conflict-resolution system, i.e., WPTL. Cf. also Douglas Roche, "A World Free of Nuclear Weapons," Chapter 14 in David Krieger, ed., The Challenge of Abolishing Nuclear Weapons, at 212: "It [a nuclear-free world] cannot wait for the peaceful resolution of conflict around the world, as if regional tranquility must be achieved before the nuclear weapon states will give up their arsenals."

62 Senator Edward Kennedy, preface to Ed Markey, Nuclear Peril: The Politics of Proliferation, at viii (1982).

63 One light-year is 5.8-trillion miles.

64 As the Jehovah Witnesses tell us, "[w]e live in a miracle." *Felicia's Journey* (1999) (Atom Egoyan, Director). Cf. also Geraint F. Lewis & Luke A. Barnes, A Fortunate Universe: Life in a Finely Tuned Cosmos (2016).

65 Cf. "How the Universe Works: Is Gravity an Illusion?" (2014) (latest physics cannot explain gravity).

66 Patti Smith, M Train, at 189 (2015). Consider even the seemingly commonplace: the weird four stages of the life of the butterfly; cows chewing their cuds multiple times to convert green grass into white milk; photosynthesis; cell biology; and trees that somehow "know" (without a brain) how tall to grow. And then there are the virtually incomprehensible mysteries of the latest cosmology, such as dark matter (meaning: "we don't know what this is"), dark energy (id), and black holes (id). See "How the Universe Works: The Dark Matter Enigma" (2017).

67 Quoted in Winslow Myers, Living Beyond War: A Citizen's Guide, at 150 (2009). Cf. id. at 151–152 (while science gave us nuclear weapons, it also gave us satellites and seismic detectors that can verify arms control treaties and technical marvels that allow increased international communication, as well as the "knowledge that international protocols of law and conflict resolution are essential to our survival").

Selected bibliography

Abolition of Nuclear Weapons

Tad Daley, Apocalypse Never: Forging the Path to a Nuclear Weapons Free World (2010).
Jon H. Else, Prod., "The Day After Trinity" documentary (1980).
Robert E. Frye, Director & Prod., "In My Lifetime" documentary (2011).
Ben Goddard, Prod., "The Nuclear Tipping Point" documentary (2010).
Errol Morris, Prod., "The Fog of War" documentary (2003).
Tanya Ogilvie-White & David Santoro, Slaying the Nuclear Dragon: Disarmament Dynamics in the Twenty-First Century (2012).
William J. Perry, My Journey at the Nuclear Brink (2015).
Douglas Roche, How We Stopped Loving the Bomb: An Insider's Account of the World on the Brink of Banning Nuclear Arms (2011).
Jonathan Schell, The Gift of Time: The Case for Abolishing Nuclear Weapons Now (1998).
Lucy Walker, Prod., "Countdown to Zero" documentary (2010).
William Walker, A Perpetual Menace: Nuclear Weapons and International Order (2012).
Lawrence Wittner, Confronting the Bomb: A Short History of the World Nuclear Disarmament Movement (2009).
Leslie Woodhead, Prod., "The Day the Bomb Dropped" documentary (2015).

Alternative Dispute Resolution

Jerome T. Barrett & Joseph P. Barrett, A History of Alternative Dispute Resolution: The Story of a Political, Cultural, and Social Movement (2004).
Melanie E. Greenberg, John H. Barton, & Margaret E. McGuiness, eds., Words Over War: Mediation and Arbitration to Prevent Deadly Conflict (2000).
J.G. Merrills, International Dispute Settlement (5th ed. 2011).
A.H.A. Soons, ed., International Arbitration: Past and Prospects (1990).
Peter Wallenstein, Understanding Conflict Resolution (3rd ed. 2012).

American Foreign Policy

Andrew J. Bacevich, The New American Militarism: How Americans are Seduced by War (2005).
———, Washington Rules: America's Path to Permanent War (2010).
James Carroll, House of War: The Pentagon and the Disastrous Rise of American Power (2006).
Stephen F. Cohen, Soviet Fates and Lost Alternatives: From Stalinism to the New Cold War (2010).
Christopher A. Preble, The Power Problem: How American Military Dominance Makes Us Less Safe, Less Prosperous, and Less Free (2009).
Philippe Sands, Lawless World: America and the Making and Breaking of Global Rules (2005).

International Economic Regulation

Ronen Palan, Richard Murphy, & Christian Chavagneux, Tax Havens: How Globalization Really Works (2010).
David Rothkopf, Power, Inc.: The Epic Rivalry between Big Business and Government—and the Reckoning That Lies Ahead (2012).
Pierre de Senarclens & Ali Kazancigil, eds., Regulating Globalization: Critical Approaches to Global Governance (2007).

International Human Rights

J. Kirk Boyd, 2048: Humanity's Agreement to Live Together: The International Movement for Enforceable Human Rights (2010).
Robert Drinan, The Mobilization of Shame: A World View of Human Rights (2001).
Paul Gordon Lauren, The Evolution of Human Rights: Visions Seen (3rd ed. 2011)(best).
Samantha Power, "A Problem from Hell": America and the Age of Genocide (2002).
Geoffrey Robertson, Crimes against Humanity: The Struggle for Global Justice (rev. ed. 2002).
Kathryn Sikkink, The Justice Cascade: How Human Rights Prosecutions Are Changing World Politics (2011).

International Law and Relations

David J. Bederman, International Law Frameworks (3rd ed. 2010).
Gleider I. Hernandez, The International Court of Justice and the Judicial Function (2014).
Mark W. Janis, America and the Law of Nations 1776–1939 (2010).

————, An Introduction to International Law (4th ed. 2003).

Mary Ellen O'Connell, The Power and Purpose of International Law: Insights from the Theory and Practice of Enforcement (2008).

Michael P. Scharf, Customary International Law in Times of Fundamental Change (2013).

Shirley V. Scott, International Law in World Politics: An Introduction (2nd ed. 2010).

Peace

Elise Boulding & Randall Forsberg, Abolishing War (1998).

Roger Chickering, Imperial Germany and a World Without War: The Peace Movement and German Society, 1892–1914 (1975).

Merle Curti, Peace or War: The American Struggle 1636–1936 (1936).

Douglas P. Fry, Beyond War: The Human Potential for Peace (2007).

Warren F. Kuehl, Seeking World Order: The United States and International Organizations to 1920 (1969).

Gerald Mische & Patricia M. Mische, Toward a Human World Order: Beyond the National Security Straitjacket (1977).

Winslow Myers, Living Beyond War: A Citizen's Guide (2009).

David S. Patterson, Toward a Warless World: The Travail of the American Peace Movement, 1887–1914 (1976).

Jonathan Schell, The Fate of the Earth (1982).

Kent D. Shifferd, From War to Peace: A Guide to the Next Hundred Years (2011).

Social Change

David Bernstein, How to Change the World: Social Entrepreneurs and the Power of New Ideas (2004).

Craig Eisendrath, At War with Time: The Wisdom of Western Thought from the Sages to a New Activism for Our Time (2003).

Adam Hochschild, Bury the Chains: Prophets and Rebels in the Fight to Free an Empire's Slaves (2005).

Nelson Mandela, Long Walk to Freedom (1994).

Samuel Moyn, The Last Utopia: Human Rights in History (2010).

Beverly Schwartz, Rippling: How Social Entrepreneurs Spread Innovation Throughout Society (2012).

Luuk Van Middelaar, The Passage to Europe: How a Continent Became a Nation (2013).

Lawrence Wittner, Confronting the Bomb: A Short History of the World Nuclear Disarmament Movement (2009).

Gordon S. Wood, Revolutionary Characters: What Made the Founders Different (2006).

United Nations and Peace Enforcement

Kofi Annan, Interventions: A Life in War and Peace (2012).

Lincoln P. Bloomfield, ed., International Military Forces: The Question of Peacekeeping in an Armed and Disarming World (1964).

Jean-Marie Guehenno, The Fog of Peace: A Memoir of International Peacekeeping in the 21st Century (2015).

Stephen C. Schlesinger, Act of Creation: The Founding of the United Nations (2003).

War and the Military

Fred Anderson & Andrew Cayton, The Dominion of War: Empire and Conflict in America, 1500–2000 (2005).

Max Boot, War Made New: Technology, Warfare, and the Course of History 1500 to Today (2006).

Michael Burleigh, Moral Combat: Good and Evil in World War II (2011).

Christopher Clark, The Sleepwalkers: How Europe Went to War in 1914 (2012).

Robert M. Gates, Duty: Memoirs of a Secretary at War (2014).

Joshua S. Goldstein, Winning the War on War: The Decline of Armed Conflict Worldwide (2011).

David Halberstam, War in a Time of Peace: Bush, Clinton, and the Generals (2001).

Shane Harris, @War: The Rise of Cyber Warfare (2014).

Adam Hochschild, To End All Wars: A Story of Loyalty and Rebellion, 1914–1918 (2011).

Kalevi J. Holsti, Peace and War: Armed Conflicts and International Order 1648–1989 (1991).

Alistair Horne, Hubris: The Tragedy of War in the Twentieth Century (2015).

G.J. Meyer, A World Undone: The Story of the Great War 1914 to 1918 (2006).

Andrew Roberts, The Storm of War: A New History of WWII (2011).

Nicholas Stargardt, The German War: A Nation Under Arms: Citizens and Soldiers, 1939–1945 (2015).

John G. Stoessinger, Why Nations Go to War (1974).

Dominic Tierney, How We Fight: Crusades, Quagmires, and the American Way of War (2010).

Adam Tooze, The Deluge: The Great War, American and the Remaking of the Global Order, 1916–1931 (2014).

Peter Turchin, War and Peace and War: The Rise and Fall of Empires (2006).

Index